Julia Weig

Lesespurgeschichten 7./8. Klasse – Englisch

Mit spannenden Geschichten differenziert Lesekompetenz fördern und nachhaltig Lust am Lesen wecken

Julia Weig hat ihr Studium an der Universität Heidelberg absolviert und ist Lehrerin an einer Gesamtschule für die Fächer Englisch und Französisch.

Wir verwenden in unseren Werken eine genderneutrale Sprache, damit sich alle gleichermaßen angesprochen fühlen. Wenn keine neutrale Formulierung möglich ist, nennen wir die weibliche und die männliche Form. In Fällen, in denen wir aufgrund einer besseren Lesbarkeit nur ein Geschlecht nennen können, achten wir darauf, den unterschiedlichen Geschlechtsidentitäten gleichermaßen gerecht zu werden.

In diesem Werk sind nach dem MarkenG geschützte Marken und sonstige Kennzeichen für eine bessere Lesbarkeit nicht besonders kenntlich gemacht. Es kann also aus dem Fehlen eines entsprechenden Hinweises nicht geschlossen werden, dass es sich um einen freien Warennamen handelt.

1. Auflage 2024

AAP Lehrerwelt GmbH
Veritaskai 3
21079 Hamburg
Telefon: +49 (0) 40325083-040
E-Mail: info@lehrerwelt.de
Geschäftsführung: Andrea Fischer, Sandra Saghbazarian
USt-ID: DE 173 77 61 42
Register: AG Hamburg HRB/126335

Autorschaft:	Julia Weig
Covergestaltung:	TSA&B Werbeagentur GmbH, Hamburg
Coverillustration:	Barbara Gerth
Illustrationen:	Barbara Gerth
Satz:	Satzpunkt Ursula Ewert GmbH, Bayreuth
Druck und Bindung:	Design and printing JSC KOPA, Kaunas

ISBN/Bestellnummer:	978-3-403-20988-1

www.persen.de

Inhaltsverzeichnis

Vorwort

Liebe Kolleginnen und Kollegen, liebe Eltern, liebe Schülerinnen und Schüler,

es freut mich sehr, dass Sie sich für dieses Heft und für die Lesespurgeschichten entschieden haben. Lesespurgeschichten sind eine tolle Möglichkeit, die **Lesekompetenz** bei Schülerinnen und Schülern zu fördern; zugleich wecken sie die **Freude am Lesen**. Für Schülerinnen und Schüler der **7. und 8. Klasse** sind sie ein nächster Schritt weg von den traditionellen Texten im Buch hin zu eigenen **Leseerfahrungen** in der Fremdsprache.

Hilfestellung zum Lesen von Lesespurgeschichten:

1: Zuerst liest man die kurze Einleitung und das Textstück Nummer 1.

2: Anschließend versucht man, durch den Hinweis im Text auf der Karte die nächste Nummer zu finden. Gelingt dies nicht direkt, kann man auch die nächsten Textabschnitte durchgucken und schauen, ob man Hinweise findet, dass hier die Geschichte weitergehen soll.

3: Dann liest man bei der nächsten Nummer weiter und schaut anschließend nochmals auf der Karte nach der nächsten Nummer. Dies wiederholt sich bis zum Schluss.

4: Findet man nicht die richtige Nummer, gibt der Textabschnitt einen deutlichen Hinweis, dass dies nicht die richtige Lesespur ist.

Differenzierung ist im Fremdsprachenunterricht ein wichtiges Thema. Aus diesem Grund liegt jede Geschichte in **zwei Niveaustufen** vor, einem einfacheren (1) und einem mittleren (2) Niveau. Das einfachere Niveau kann beispielsweise auch problemlos in der Real- oder Hauptschule eingesetzt werden. Die Textabschnitte des mittleren Niveaus sind etwas ausführlicher, verfügen über einen anspruchsvolleren Wortschatz und haben zusätzlich noch eingebaute Rätsel, die die Schülerinnen und Schüler lösen müssen.

Es empfiehlt sich, die erste Lesespurgeschichte mit den Schülerinnen und Schülern gemeinsam zu bearbeiten, damit ihnen das Format vertraut ist. Anschließend kann man sie die nächsten Geschichten problemlos **allein** oder in **Partnerarbeit** lösen lassen. Sie haben als Lehrkraft dann verschiedene **Kontrollmöglichkeiten**: Die Schülerinnen und Schüler können allein mithilfe der Lösungsseite kontrollieren, sie besprechen die richtige Lesespur gemeinsam am Ende im Plenum oder die Schülerinnen und Schüler kontrollieren sich gegenseitig mit der Sitznachbarin bzw. dem Sitznachbarn.

In der Vergangenheit hat sich herausgestellt, dass Lesespurgeschichten dadurch **verschiedene Lese- und Lerntypen** ansprechen, dass sie nicht nur Text enthalten, sondern der Text mit dem Entdecken der Spur auf der Karte kombiniert ist.

Gutes Gelingen und viel Spaß beim Lösen der Geschichten wünscht

Julia Weig

Chasing a thief in New York City
Lesespurlandkarte

Chasing a thief in New York City
Lesespurgeschichte (1)

Sam spent the last summer holidays in New York where he was visiting his uncle George, his aunt Ella und his cousin Peter. Sam and Peter like each other a lot and were very happy to have two weeks and a lot of time for nice activities together! One day they took the subway to Central Park because they wanted to row a boat on the lake there. While they were on the stairs to leave the subway station there was a tumult behind them.

If you want to know what happened, start reading at number 1.

1 The two boys only heard some loud noises and people screaming. There were people running in different directions creat**i**$_4$ng a busy atmosphere. What had just happened? Then Sam realised that his phone was gone! Was it somewhere on the floor? He looked around! No! It must have been stolen! "Peter", he shouted, "my phone is gone! Sh…" The escalator went up into the daylight and they stood aside. You could see Peter's shoulders hanging and his sad face. Sam's phone was new and expensive! "Oh no, that can't be true! Keep calm, we'll find it! Let's call my dad and mum first and tell them what happened … maybe they have an idea." Peter said. "What's that behind you? Peter we need to be quick! I see somebody running away over there! Let's follow him! QUIIIIIICK!!!!!"

2 Another famous building in Manhattan is the so called "Flatiron Building", it got its name because of the shape. Today, several companies have their office in this building. Buildings which are used as offices usually have security people who see to it that nobody enters who is not allowed to do so. Many of them also have electronic doors which can be locked quickly in case of an emergency. That's why hiding in this building would not be a clever idea, so please go on searching the next location.

3 The race in Central Park continued! Sam wanted to get back his new smartphone because he had saved a lot of money that he got from his grandparents for Christmas and his last two birthdays to buy it. Besides, all his memories from the trip to New York, all the photos he had taken so far were on this phone! He couldn't even imagine losing all these pictures! The boys **f**$_3$ollowed the thief who was now running around the lake in Central Park. "Hey, that's where we actually wanted to go! It looks pretty nice, I hope we can still do that", Sam shouted to Peter who could only nod because he was so out of breath.

4 Peter was a bit stressed when Sam started running so quickly – he is a very fast runner. Peter is rather a relaxed person and doesn't like running fast, but he gave his best and tried to follow his cousin. They started running past a small Indian supermarket towards Central Park. Outside the supermarket there were several people who were looking around. The two boys nearly crashed into an old lady who started screaming at them.

5 When going towards the harbour in New York, tourists can see some ships and a few shops and restaurants on the promenade. Every day the market hall at the harbour is crowded because it is famous for its fresh food. Inside, it smells like fish and some people feel like throwing up when they enter. You can see shop assistants everywhere shouting for instance: "Buy two kilos of bananas and get two oranges for free!" As the market hall is pretty crowded and people are walking around slowly searching the best offer, it is not a good place to rush through when escaping with a stolen object. Moreover, the thief does not pass this area of Manhattan, so please go on searching the next location.

6 They were wrong because the thief changed his direction and did not go to Brooklyn. Sam and Peter were relieved! They were about to spot another place with a lot of shimmering lights! But that was not Chinatown, no, it was TIMES SQUARE! "That's a very special place!", Sam thought. It has always been his dream to stand on this square and buy tickets for a musical. Then they saw him again! There he was, climbing up the stairs. "How stupid of a thief, up there everybody can see him", Sam thought. He climbed up the stairs and realised that he could not run down the other side. "That's our chance", Peter screamed. "We can catch him!" The two boys tried to stop the thief when he ran back down the stairs. They nearly got him but he somehow managed to continue his way to different stairs.

7 The thief ran up the stairs again. Sam is a very good sportsman, but they were close to giving up because they were so exhausted. They followed him up the stairs … what a beautiful view of the houses in this area of New York. Normally Sam would have stopped here to take lots of pictures, but that was impossible without his new phone. Up here was a small path with nice plants on the left and on the right, they could see people sitting on benches enjoying the view or reading newspapers and books. "That's the High Line", Peter explained, "after we catch this thie**f**$_2$ we'll come back to this place and enjoy the nice atmosphere. It's one of my favourite places to escape the busy city."

8 Escaping into a department store would be a great idea! For a thief that would definitely be a good option because it is very crowded so you can easily hide. There are a lot of different levels and several doors through which you can escape. A famous department store in New York and in the US is Macy's where you can buy nearly everything: clothes, shoes, books, jewelry … and so on. Every day there are a lot of people and tourists going for a shopping trip and if you are hungry, you can also find something to eat there. The thief who stole Sam's phone did not have this great idea and didn't pass by Macy's, so please go on searching the next location.

9 You've just arrived at the Empire State Building: a skyscraper in Manhattan built in 1930 and until 1970 it was the highest building in the world. This is probably only one of the reasons why so many tourists visit this building every year. Standing up on the platform you have a great view of the whole city and you can take cool pictures! Visiting the Empire State Building is definitely on Sam's bucket list for his trip to New York but right now their chase of the thief doesn't lead them here. Please go back to the last location where Sam and Peter have seen the thief.

10 Up on the street the boys heard a police siren. Where was the thief? They looked left and right and behind the police car they suddenly heard voices! "You better stop moving like that or we'll directly bring you to prison!", a policeman called. "Sir!", Sam shouted gasping, "this man has just stolen my new smartphone. We followed him around the whole city and here we are now. How did you know that he is a thief, and why did you catch him?" "I knew it! He was running so quickly, bumping into people and we thought that he must be running away from somebody. And now we know, he was escaping from you guys! It was very brave of you to follow him but also very risky, he could have attacked you with a knife or something else. Do promise me, next time you'll directly call the police." "Yes, of course, we will, officer! Thank you!", the boys replied.

11 Luckily, they could escape the lady without being hit. ☺ Central Park is so big and every day there are lots of tourists lying in the grass, having a chat and enjoying the good atmosphere. The two boys ran past these tourists still following the thief who had his difficulties not to bump into people. The thief was quick! Impressive! Peter had difficulties following him, as running is not his strong point. Sam, until now, managed without any major problems. From behind they saw that the thief nearly ran into a young girl who was about to throw an old banana in a dustbin. "Hey, be careful! You nearly crashed into me", the girl shouted!

12 This is the impressive and huge "MoMa", the Museum of Modern Art in New York. Sam is not too interested in art and only goes to the museum when either his parents or his teachers force him to. So when he has the choice, he will definitely not spend an afternoon in a museum, especially not in summer when it's sunny outside and there are so many better options to choose from. So please go back to the last place and continue searching the way where the thief has escaped.

13 Here you are in front of a hot dog stall in Central Park where you can see a huge queue every day! No wonder, these hot dogs are so popular – they are just delicious. Sam was extremely hungry, but they just didn't have the time to stop here and get hot dogs. They would have to postpone that. Later they could come here, get some hot dogs and a milkshake. Right now, they have to continue chasing the thief so please go back to the last stop.

14 You are pretty cl**o**$_1$se, the thief ran inside an Asian restaurant but that one was Chinese. Here you are in front of a Japanese sushi place with a large smiling fish painted on the front of the building. Peter doesn't really like sushi. Why the hell is it so expensive? Last year, he tried sushi for the first time when his aunt was visiting because sushi is her favourite food. So please go back to the last stop and search for the correct restaurant the thief has escaped into.

15 This is the harbour where the ferry boats leave. A lot of tourists in New York take the Staten Island Ferry for a trip because the ferry goes past the Statue of Liberty so you have a nice view of the statue getting pretty close to it without paying. The area around the harbour is also very crowded every day since there are local people from New York taking the ferry to go to work for example. Here it would be difficult to find a person, in this case the thief, so Sam and Peter are happy that he doesn't run to this area. Please go back to the last location and continue searching.

16 Right now you have arrived at one of the coffee shops in New York. A lot of people get a "**c**$_5$offee to go" in the morning because they work late hours and do not have time to prepare a coffee themselves. Sam and Peter don't like drinking coffee but they like going to these coffee shops to get some fresh lemonade, shakes or muffins – they have a huge variety to choose from and everything is delicious. Today they don't have time to stop by since they are following the thief and moreover the thief didn't pass this coffee shop. Please continue searching somewhere else.

17 The thief ran around the whole lake in Central Park and left the park through a huge old gate. This gate looked like it's from an old film from the 1920s with lots of beautiful ornaments. Back on the street the boys suddenly had the impression that the thief managed to escape! Where was he? They couldn't see him anymore! They were standing at a huge crossing with roads leading in four different directions and a lot of cars and people around. So they had four options to follow but what if they chose the wrong direction? The thief would be gone! They were discussing which way to choose when Peter shouted that a few metres down the road to the left he heard people shouting and discussing. That must be the direction!

18 This huge and beautiful building right in front is the Grand Central Terminal, one of Peter's favourite buildings and places in town. He has always liked the atmosphere which you can feel at train stations or airports. Sometimes he just likes coming here looking at people saying goodbye to each other or welcoming others after, maybe, a long time. These situations were so heartwarming. The Grand Central Terminal is huge! For this reason, the two boys are lucky that the thief didn't run here. Go on searching somewhere else.

19 The race continued down the stairs back into the busy traffic of the city. The thief crossed the street even though there was a red light and an old pick-up truck nearly crashed into him. The driver honked a few times. As the thief did not react, he stuck his head out of the window and starting shouting at him: "Hey man, are you crazy? You had a red light! I nearly killed you, you could have been dead!" Sam and Peter saw this whole scene from above while they were running down the stairs of the High Line. But the thief ignored the pick-up driver and just continued his way. "Jesus, Peter, that was a dangerous situation. The pick-up driver could have killed him", Sam said. "Y**e**$_6$s of course, I would have been happy if the driver had been able to stop this guy. I am close to collapsing I cannot continue a long time anymore", Peter replied. "Where is he going? I see red, green and white flags everywhere. Is this an Irish quarter over here?" Sam asked. "No", Peter smiled. "That's Little Italy." The boys continued as the thief passed some Italian restaurants with people sitting in front of them in the sun having lunch. At the back of one street, he jumped down some stairs into a subway tunnel.

20 In front of you, there is the ve**r**$_7$y famous Rockefeller Center. You have probably already seen the famous Christmas tree standing in front of it in December. In wintertime, there are also many people ice-skating in front of the building. It must be an awesome feeling! The Rockefeller Center is a popular sight for tourists because of the observation deck "Top of the Rock" at the top. From there you have a nice view of the city. On top of the Empire State Building the view is great as well but on the Rockefeller Center you also have the Empire State Building in your pictures which makes it even nicer.

21 In Manhattan there are also several churches. A famous one is St. Patrick's Cathedral, a Catholic church in Midtown Manhattan, close to Rockefeller Center. This means that our thief could definitely pass by this church and try to hide. Hiding in a church is not a clever idea since it closes in the night and then the thief would be locked in there. During the day there are a lot of tourists inside, so hiding would also not be easy. So please go on searching the thief somewhere else.

22 At the back of the **s**$_{8}$treet where the noise of the people had come from, they could see red, yellowish and orange lights and huge signs with Chinese characters that they did not understand. That must be Chinatown! They went on following the direction where the noise had come from and then Sam finally saw him again! He entered a Chinese restaurant with a huge waving cat in the shop window. The thief passed through the restaurant and left it through the back door! From Chinatown southwards you can see the huge Brooklyn Bridge which connects Manhattan and Brooklyn. During the day there are a lot of tourists taking pictures for their Instagram stories. Then Peter suddenly spotted the thief! He was running through the crowds and bumping into some young Asian looking girls. Was he escaping to Brooklyn? No way! They had no choice but to follow him.

23 In the tunnel he ran on the platform. When Peter and Sam came down into the subway tunnel, they saw train A which goes to Williamsburg standing on the tracks. Their eyes searched the train, the platform, the benches on the platform. Where was the thief? Had he entered the train? "Oh no, let's hope he didn't get in the train and escape to Williamsburg, we will never find him there", Peter said. Then suddenly a man jumped out from a snack vending machine … he must have hidden there for a few seconds! He continued his way and left the subway station at the back of the platform. Sam and Peter followed him!

My reading trail:

1										

Solution word: The New York City Police Department (NYPD) is the largest and one of the oldest in the United States. The NYPD headquarters is at 1 Police Plaza, located on Park Row in Lower Manhattan near City Hall. The NYPD employs around 55,000 people, including almost 35,000 uniformed ....

Vocabulary

to go rowing	Rudern gehen	**exhausted**	erschöpft
emergency	Notfall	**department store**	Kaufhaus
to chase	jagen, verfolgen	**to honk**	hupen
thief	Dieb	**obstacle**	Hindernis
to throw up	sich übergeben	**to postpone**	verschieben
impressive	beeindruckend	**ornament**	Ziergegenstand

Chasing a thief in New York City
Lesespurgeschichte (2)

Sam spent the last summer holidays in New York where he was visiting his uncle George, his aunt Ella und his cousin Peter. Sam and Peter like each other a lot and were very happy to have two weeks and a lot of time for nice activities together! One day they took the subway to Central Park because they wanted to row a boat on the lake there. While they were on the stairs to leave the subway station there was a tumult behind them.

If you want to know what happened, start reading at number 1.

1 The two boys only heard some loud noises and people screami**i**$_4$ng. There were people running in different directions creating a busy atmosphere. What had just happened? Sam touched his right thigh and realised that his phone was gone! Did he just drop it? Was it somewhere on the floor? He looked around! No! It must have been stolen! "Peter", he shouted, "my phone is gone! Sh…" He was paralyzed and couldn't believe it. The escalator went up into the daylight and they stood aside. Peter made a sad face. Sam's phone was new and expensive. "Oh no, that can't be true! Keep calm, we'll find it! Let's call my dad and mum first and tell them what happened … maybe they have an idea", Peter said. "What's that behind you? Peter we need to be quick! I see somebody running away over there! Let's follow him! QUIIIIIICK!!!!!"

2 Another famous building in Manhattan is the so called "Flatiron Building", it got its name because of the shape, as it is a triangular 22-story house. Completed in 1902, the name "Flatiron" comes from its resemblance to a clothes iron. Today, several companies have their office in this building. Buildings which are used as offices usually have security people who see to it that nobody enters who is not allowed to do so. Many of them also have electronic doors which can be locked quickly in case of an emergency. These are many reasons why hiding in or escaping into this building would not be a clever idea, so please go on searching the next location.

3 The race in Central Park continued! The boys felt a bit like in an old CSI Miami film chasing thieves around the city! Sam wanted to get back his new smartphone because he had saved a lot of money that he received from his grandparents for Christmas and his last two birthdays to buy it. Besides, all his memories from the trip to New York, all the photos he had taken so far were on this phone! He couldn't even imagine losing all these pictures, but why hasn't he saved them in between, like for example uploaded them in the cloud? He would learn from this mistake for the next trip! The boys **f**$_3$ollowed the thief who was now running around the lake in Central Park. "Hey, that's where we actually wanted to go! It looks pretty nice, I hope we can still do that", Sam shouted to Peter who could only nod because he was so out of breath.

4 Peter was a bit overwhelmed when Sam started running so quickly – he is a very fast runner. Peter is rather a relaxed person and doesn't like running fast, but he gave his best and tried to follow his cousin. They started running past a small Indian supermarket towards Central Park. Outside the supermarket there were several shelves with fruits and fresh herbs and some people were looking around trying to find what they wanted to buy. The two boys nearly crashed into an old lady with a walking stick who started screaming at them pointing with the stick in their direction.

5 When going towards the harbor in New York, tourists can see some ships and a few shops and restaurants on the promenade. One can also spot "Bubba Gump Shrimp Shop" which is related to the famous "Forest Gump" film! Every day the market hall at the harbor is crowded because it is famous for its fresh food. Inside, it smells like fish and some people feel like throwing up when they enter. You can see shop assistants everywhere shouting for instance: "Buy two kilos of bananas and get two oranges for free!" – "Today special offer – the best tuna in New York has just arrived from Tokyo! Only 35$ per kilo!" As the market hall is very crowded and people are walking around slowly searching the best offer, it is not a good place to rush through when escaping with a stolen object. Moreover, the thief does not pass this area of Manhattan, so please go on searching the next location.

6 They were wrong because the thief changed his direction and did not go to Brooklyn. Sam and Peter were relieved! They were about to spot another place with a lot of shimmering lights! But that was not Chinatown, no, it was TIMES SQUARE! Times Square with all its shining adverts high above people's heads. "That's a very special place!", Sam thought. It has always been his dream to stand on this square and buy tickets for a musical at the small stall next to the big stairs. Then he suddenly saw the thief climbing up the stairs! "How stupid of a thief, up there everybody can see him", Sam thought. Well, obviously our thief was not the smartest person but he was in a stressful situation. He climbed up the stairs and realised that he could not run down the other side. "That's our chance", Peter screamed. "We can catch him!" The two boys tried to stop the thief when he ran back down the stairs. They nearly got him, Sam even grabbed his arm but he was strong and could tear himself off to continue his way to different stairs.

7 The thief ran up the stairs again. Wow, he is in a really good physical condition! Sam is also a very good sportsman, but they were close to giving up because they were so exhausted. They followed him up the stairs … what a beautiful view of the red brick houses in this area of New York. Sam loved this architectural style and normally he would have stopped here to take lots of pictures, but that was impossible without his beloved new phone. Up here was a small path with nice plants on the left and on the right, they could see people sitting on benches enjoying the view or reading newspapers and books. "That's the High Line", Peter explained, "when we catch this bloody thie**f**$_2$, we'll come back to this place and enjoy the nice atmosphere. It's one of my favourite places to escape the hustle and bustle of the busy city."

8 Escaping into a department store would be a great idea! For a thief that would definitely be a smart option because it is very crowded so you can easily hide. Besides there are a lot of different levels and several entrance and exit doors through which you can escape. A famous department store in New York and in the US is "Macy's" where you can buy pretty much everything: clothes, shoes, books, jewelry and so on. Every day there are a lot of people and tourists going for a shopping trip and if you are hungry, you can also find something to eat there. The thief who stole Sam's phone did not have this great idea and thus didn't pass by "Macy's", so please go on searching the next location.

9 You've just arrived at the Empire State Building: a 102-story skyscraper in Manhattan built in 1930 and until 1970 it was the highest building in the world. This is probably only one of the reasons why so many tourists visit this building every year. Standing up on the platform you have a great view of the whole city and you can take breathtaking pictures! Visiting the Empire State Building is definitely on Sam's bucket list for his trip to New York but right now their chase of the thief doesn't lead them here. Please go back to the last location where Sam and Peter have seen the thief.

In New York, there are a lot of skyscrapers and high-rise buildings, but where can you find the tallest building in the world (2024)?

a) New York

b) Shanghai

c) Dubai

10 Up on the street the boys heard a police siren. Where was the thief? They looked left and right and behind the police car they suddenly heard voices! "You better stop moving like that or we'll directly bring you to prison!", a policeman called in a harsh tone. "Sir!", Sam shouted gasping, "this man has just stolen my new smartphone. We followed him around the whole city and here we are now. How did you know that he is a thief, and why did you catch him?" "I knew it! He was running so quickly, bumping into people and it looked suspicious to us as if he was fleeing from somebody. And now we know, he was escaping from you guys! It was very brave of you to follow him but also very risky, he could have attacked you with a knife or any other weapon. Do promise me, next time you'll directly call the police." "Yes, of course, we will, officer! Thank you!", the boys replied.

11 Luckily, they could escape the lady without being hit. ☺ Central Park is overwhelmingly huge and probably the biggest park Sam has ever been to! Every day there are lots of tourists lying in the grass, having a chat and enjoying the good atmosphere, probably resting after exhausting tourist activities downtown. The two boys ran past these tourists still following the thief who had his difficulties not to bump into people crossing his way. The thief was quick! Has he already run a marathon?! Impressive! Peter had difficulties following him, as running is not his strong point, but Sam, until now, managed without any major problems. From behind they saw that the thief nearly ran into a young girl who was about to throw an old banana peel in a dustbin. "Hey, be careful! You nearly crashed into me", the girl shouted! What if the thief had slipped on the banana? That would have been funny and the end of our chase. Sam imagined. But unfortunately, the thief was clever and got past his obstacle!

Calculate the area of Central Park: length 4 km from 59th Street to 110th Street and 0.8 km wide between 5th Avenue and Central Park West.

The total area of Central Park is ………………………………………………………………………………………….

12 This is the impressive and huge "MoMa", the Museum of Modern Art in New York. Sam is not too interested in art and only goes to the museum when either his parents or his teachers force him to. So when he has the choice, he will definitely not spend an afternoon in a museum, especially not in summer when it's sunny outside and there are so many better options to choose from. So please go back to the last place and continue searching the way where the thief has escaped.

13 Here you are in front of a hot dog stall in Central Park where you can see a huge queue every day! No wonder, these hot dogs are so popular – they are just delicious. Sam had already thought about his hunger for a while and running consumed a lot of energy, but they just didn't have the time to stop here and get hot dogs. They would have to postpone that. After the chase they could come here, get some hot dogs and a milkshake. Right now, they have to continue chasing the thief so please go back to the last stop.

14 You are pretty close, the thief ran into an Asian restaurant but that one was Chinese. Here you are in front of a Japanese sushi place with a large smiling fish painted on the front of the building. Peter had heard that it is supposed to be a pretty good restaurant, but sushi is something he has never liked and does not want to spend so much money on raw fish. Why the hell is it so expensive? Last year, he tried sushi for the first time when his aunt was visiting because sushi is her favourite food. So please go back to the last stop and search for the correct restaurant the thief has escaped into.

15 This is the harbour where the ferry boats leave. A lot of tourists in New York take the Staten Island Ferry for a trip because the ferry goes past the Statue of Liberty. So you have a nice view of the statue getting pretty close to it without paying for it. The area around the harbour is also very crowded every day since there are local people from New York taking the ferry to go to work for example. Here it would be difficult to find a person, in this case the thief, so Sam and Peter are happy that he doesn't run to this area. Please go back to the last location and continue searching.

16 Right now you have arrived at one of the shops of a big American coffee chain with shops all around the world. Getting a "**c**$_5$offee to go" in the morning is a pretty common thing in America since a lot of people work late hours and do not have time to prepare a coffee themselves. And who doesn't need his daily dose of caffeine? Sam and Peter don't like drinking coffee (yet) but they like going to these coffee shops to get some fresh lemonade, frappé shakes or muffins – they have a huge variety to choose from and everything is simply delicious. Today they don't have time to stop by since they are following the thief and moreover the thief didn't pass this coffee shop. Please continue searching somewhere else.

17 The thief ran around the whole lake in Central Park and then left the park through a huge old gate. Sam and Peter had to hurdle between boats and rowing equipment lying around next to the small lake house, but they always managed to keep an eye on the thief and not lose his track. The gate looked like it's from an old film from the 1920s with lots of beautiful ornaments. Back on the street the boys suddenly had the impression that the thief managed to escape! Where was he? They couldn't see him anymore! They were standing at a huge crossing with roads leading in four different directions and a lot of cars, vans and people around. So they basically had four options to follow but what if they chose the wrong one? The thief would be gone and Sam didn't even dare to finish this thought. They were discussing which way to choose when Peter shouted that a few metres down the road to the left he heard people shouting and complaining. That must be the direction and the thief must have bumped into innocent people walking around!

18 This huge and beautiful building right in front is the Grand Central Terminal, one of Peter's favourite buildings and places in town. He has always liked the busy atmosphere which you can feel and observe at train stations or airports. Sometimes he just likes coming here looking at people saying goodbye to each other or welcoming others after, supposedly, a long time. These situations were so heartwarming! The Grand Central Terminal has more than 50 passenger tracks and it's huge. For this reason, the two boys are lucky that the thief didn't run here. Go on searching somewhere else.

British vs. American English! Do you know the American English word corresponding to the British one?

British English	American English
pavement	
colour	
biscuit	
film	
flat	

19 The race continued down the stairs back into the busy traffic of the city. The thief crossed the street even though the pedestrians had a red light and an old pick-up truck nearly crashed into him. The driver braked and honked a few times. As the thief did not react, he stuck his head out of the window and starting shouting at him: "Hey man, are you crazy? You had a red light! I nearly killed you! Do you know the traffic regulations??! I think you don't!" Sam and Peter witnessed this whole scene from above while they were running down the stairs of the High Line. But the thief ignored the pick-up driver and just continued his way. "Jesus, Peter, that was a dangerous situation. The pick-up driver could have killed him", Sam said. "Y**e**$_{6}$s of course, I would have been happy if the driver had been able to stop this guy. I am close to collapsing I cannot continue a long time anymore", Peter replied. "Where is he going? I see red, green and white flags everywhere. Is this an Irish quarter over here?", Sam asked. "No", Peter smiled. "That's Little Italy. A quarter which was founded by Italian immigrants who came to the US in the 19th century." The boys continued as the thief passed some Italian restaurants with people sitting in front of them in the sun having lunch. At the back of one street, he jumped down some stairs into a subway tunnel.

20 In front of you, there is the ve**r**$_{7}$y famous Rockefeller Center. You have probably already seen the famous Christmas tree standing in front of it during the festive season in December. In wintertime, there are also many people ice-skating on the territory of the building. Ice-skating while being surrounded by so many skyscrapers must be an awesome feeling! The Rockefeller Center is a popular sight for tourists coming to New York throughout the whole year because of the observation deck "Top of the Rock" at the top from which you have a nice view of the city. On top of the Empire State Building the view is great as well but when standing on the Rockefeller Center you also have the Empire State Building in your pictures which makes it even better.

21 In Manhattan there are also several churches and one of the more famous ones is St. Patrick's Cathedral, a Catholic church in Midtown Manhattan, close to Rockefeller Center. This means that our thief could definitely pass by this church and try to hide. Hiding in a church is not a clever idea since it closes in the night and then the thief would be locked in there. During the day there are a lot of tourists inside, so hiding would also not be easy. Besides, the 19 church bells are tolling regularly which might be annoying, right? So please go on searching the thief somewhere else.

22 At the back of the **s**$_8$treet where the noise of the people had come from, they could see red, yellowish and orange lights and huge signs with Chinese characters that they did not understand. That must be Chinatown! They went on following the direction where the noise had come from and then Sam finally saw him again! He entered a Chinese restaurant with a huge waving cat in the window. Sam was starving, for the only food he had had today was a sesame bagel with cream cheese (a typical American breakfast ☺) but they had to continue running after the thief. The thief passed through the restaurant and left it through the back door! From Chinatown southwards you can see the huge Brooklyn Bridge which connects the New York boroughs of Manhattan and Brooklyn. During the day the bridge is populated with immense crowds of tourists taking pictures for their Instagram stories. Then Peter suddenly spotted the thief! There he was paving his way through the crowds of tourists and bumping into some young Asian looking girls. Was he escaping to Brooklyn? No way! They had no choice but to follow him.

23 In the tunnel he ran on the platform. When Peter and Sam came down into the subway tunnel, they saw train A which goes to Williamsburg standing on the tracks. Their eyes searched the train, the platform, the benches on the platform. Where was the thief? Had he entered the train? "Oh no, let's hope he didn't get in the train and escape to Williamsburg, we will never find him there and I also don't have the best sense of orientation in places that I have rarely been to", Peter said. Then suddenly a man jumped out from a snack vending machine … he must have hidden there for a few seconds! He continued his way and left the subway station at the back of the platform. Sam and Peter followed him!

My reading trail:	1										

Solution word: The New York City Police Department (NYPD) is the largest and one of the oldest in the United States. The NYPD headquarters is at 1 Police Plaza, located on Park Row in Lower Manhattan near City Hall. The NYPD employs around 55,000 people, including almost 35,000 uniformed ....

Chasing a thief in New York City
Lösungen

My reading trail:	1	4	11	3	17	22	6	7	19	23	10

Solution word: **officers**

Solutions:

Riddle to **9**: The tallest building in the world can be found in **Dubai** (2024), it's the Burj Khalifa.

Riddle to **11**: The area of Central Park is approximately **3,2 km² (exact area 3,41 km²).**

Riddle to **18**: British vs. American English! Do you know the American English word corresponding to the British one?

British English	American English
pavement	**sidewalk**
colour	**color**
biscuit	**cookie**
film	**movie**
flat	**apartment**

At the airport
Lesespurlandkarte

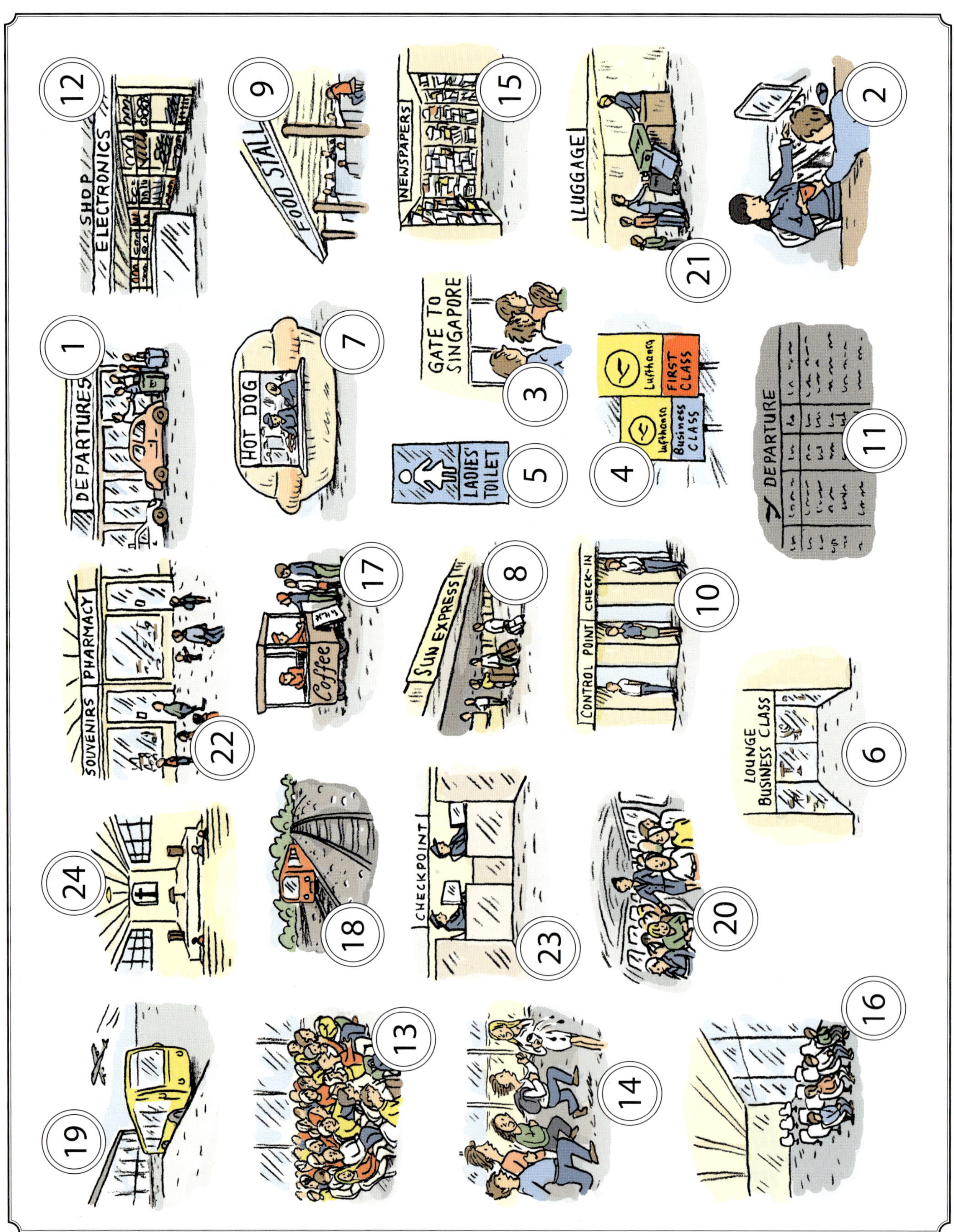

At the airport
Lesespurgeschichte (1)

Julie and her family planned to fly to San Francisco in the summer holidays and do a road trip in California with a camper van. It was her first longer flight and that's why she was extremely nervous and did not know what to expect. Her older brother Peter had already been to the US with their uncle, so he was an expert when it came to longer flights.

If you want to know what Julie experienced at the airport, start reading at number 1.

1 The Germaine family had two large suitcases and a smaller one. Julie had to share a suitcase with her mother because her parents told her that they would take the subway from the airport to the hotel in San Francisco. Afterwards they also had to walk about 15 minutes, so she was not allowed to take too much stuff with her for the time in California. As the suitcases were heavy, Julie's uncle drove the family to the airport by car. They arrived at the entrance and uncle Jim left.

2 After some long minutes the queue was gone and it was their turn. Julie's parents showed all the four passports to the lady working there. In Julie's eyes she looked very important. The lady printed the boarding passes for the four of them. "Oh we don't need them", Mr Germaine said. "I have all the boarding passes in the wallet on my phone. I think this is quite useful because we are saving paper." "George, stop telling the woman our whole life story. Take the boarding passes, they are useful because we can give them to Julie and Peter. In case they get lost, they will know where to go, people can help them find us or they can even board the plane without us."

3 This is the gate where the plane to Singapore is going to board soon. Julie's parents had always wanted to fly to Singapore but with the heat there in August they decided to fly to California instead. They were sure that San Francisco and the national parks would be an exciting experience for Julie and her brother. But one day, they will definitely go to Singapore to have a look at the amazing Marina Bay Sands and the Gardens by the Bay. So this is not the correct gate, go back to the last place and search the right one.

4 This is not the correct entrance for the hand luggage check and the passenger screening. This is the entrance for business and first class passengers. Julie's dad had checked the prices for a business class ticket because he always had problems to fit into the seat in the economy class because his legs are so long! But the prices were too high. In the end, they decided that they don't want to spend so much money on a plane ticket but that it makes more sense to use it for activities in California with the whole family. So that's why they don't use this entrance today, please go back to the last place.

5 After Peter got his hot dog, the family continued their way through the airport building. "Peter, be careful!! You are making a mess with your ketchup! See, there is some of it on our new suitcase!" – "Ah, come on, don't worry! At least, we will recognise the suitcase on the baggage carousel hahaha! There are always so many suitcases or bags which look exactly the same and it gets pretty difficult to find yours." "Peter, stop talking, we need to move on! But first I'll need a toilet …", Mrs Germaine shouted. So the whole family moved in the direction of the toilets.

6 This is not the correct room. This is the lounge where the business class passengers can eat something before their flight. Julie saw expensive looking bottles and tables with nice decoration and fresh flowers. "One day, I'll also be able to get into this lounge before I go on a business trip", she dreamed. Today she has to go on finding the gate for her flight, so please go on searching the next place.

7 Of course, it's always like that! Julie knew it! As soon as they enter the airport building, Peter shouts "Muuuuum, daaaaad, I'm hungry, I need something to eat!" "Oh no, Peter, why are you ALWAYS hungry?", Julie replied. "My dear little sister, I am two years older than you are, plus I am 20 cm taller than you AND I am still growing. Over there is a bakery, I'll get myself a hot dog. That's perfect to get in the right mood for our stay in the US."

8 When you come to the airport there are many different counters of many different airlines. Air Austria, Delta, United, Quantas … Unfortunately, this is not the correct desk to drop off the luggage of the Germaine family. This is the counter of SunExpress, an airline only offering flights in Europe and not to the US … Please look for the correct airline and go back to the last place.

9 At this food stall you can only buy fast food: burgers, fries, grilled cheese sandwiches … No, Julie is not allowed to eat so much fast food. Only from time to time her mum makes an exception. And wow, this food is also very expensive! That's incredible. The prices are about one third higher than in the city centre, Julie realised. "Probably that's normal at the airport", she thought. So please find the correct spot where Julie can get healthier food and go back to the last place.

10 When they found out that their flight to San Francisco would be leaving from gate C27 they went to the control point where all passengers were checked and screened along with the hand luggage. Again, the next line. "When you go to an airport, you have to stand in line a lot", Julie thought. She wanted to keep on looking forward to her great trip to California! Julie was very ticklish and had to laugh when the lady screened her body with the stick. At the same time, she felt safer because of this detailed control.

11 Julie held her boarding pass in her hands and was so happy! She was so much looking forward to this trip and the long flight. She had heard that everybody can watch their own film during the flight. What kind of films would they have this time? She hoped that she could see the romantic comedy which had just premiered a few weeks ago. Now the whole family was standing in front of the huge sign indicating the departure times and the gates for all the flights around the world. And everybody was searching their flight BA287 to San Francisco.

12 This is a shop where you can buy all sorts of electronic devices: headphones, mobile phones, chargers, loudspeakers … That's a paradise for Peter and Julie's mum because they love technology! When the family passes such a shop It's always difficult for Mr Germaine to prevent them from spending lots of money for things they already have. Mr Germaine thinks the old equipment should be used until it doesn't work anymore. Today he is lucky, his wife and his son don't even see the shop.

13 In front of this gate Julie sees two football teams, a female and a male one both wearing their team jerseys. Where are they going? Against which team will they be playing there? Both teams were pretty loud and suddenly started to cheer when the plane was ready to board. Julie was happy that the teams were not on her plane. She prefers a quiet flight so she can watch nice films. As this is not the correct gate of Julie's flight, please continue searching the next place.

14 After the passport check the four of them walked in the direction of their gate which was next to a big shelf with newspapers from all over the world. Mr Germaine started looking at them taking a French and a German newspaper for the long flight. "Oh noooooo", Mrs Germaine sighed, "we are at the wrong gate, they changed it. Let's get up and hurry up, we need to get to a different part of the building." How stressful … they started running! Peter bumped into a young lady who nearly dropped her coffee-to-go cup. "Sooooorrry", he shouted quickly and they all continued their way.

15 Of course. In front of the ladies' toilet there was a long queue! Peter and Mr Germaine quickly walked into the men's toilet and left it after a short while, but Mrs Germaine had to wait for minutes. She was already getting nervous because it was quite urgent. In the meantime, Julie was keeping an eye on the family's luggage while looking at a small kiosk with books and newspapers. She was proud that her parents trusted her with guarding the luggage. She bought a crime novel for the flight since she didn't know if she would like the films on board of the airplane.

16 When the Germaine family finally arrived at the correct gate, they were all out of breath and stressed. They sat down and started waiting, Julie read her novel and Peter checked messages on his phone. Just seconds later, the employees of the airline made an announcement explaining that boarding would be done in different groups. At the beginning first and business class passengers and families travelling with young children under the age of 6 were allowed to board the plane. "They do it like this to avoid chaos on board and that not everybody rushes inside at the same time", Peter explained. Julie was annoyed by her older brother and just looked at her ticket realising that they were group two meaning they would soon be allowed to enter the plane.

17 This is a little food stall only selling coffee: cappuccino, espresso, latte … and obviously there were a lot of tired people at the airport because there was a loooooong queue. Many people standing in line there were wearing suits or business dresses and looked like they were travelling for work. Julie thought that it must be exhausting to do so many business trips. She prefers travelling for private reasons. Besides, she doesn't drink coffee yet and doesn't start queuing here.

18 In front of you is the entrance for the train to go to terminal 2. Since the airport of London Heathrow is huge, there is more than one terminal and some airlines only operate from the other terminals. So passengers sometimes have to take the little train to get to the other building of the airport. Julie thought it would be fun to take this train but today they already arrived at the correct terminal. Hopefully next time! This means you have to go back to the last place.

19 Some gates do not have a direct access to the plane, but you need to take another bus which takes you to your plane. Every year there are more and more people flying around the world and that's why the airports sometimes cannot park all the planes right in front of the building. Last year when Julie flew to Spain, she had to take such a bus. Today they don't need one, their plane has direct access to the building. That's why this is not the correct place.

20 Inside the plane, when they had put their small suitcase in the shelf above their heads and the rucksack underneath the seat in front of them, they all started relaxing finally. This morning at the airport had been more stressful than expected! The stewards explained the security guidelines. In the meantime, Julie checked the board entertainment system and was super happy when she realised that she could watch her beloved rom-com. Now, finally the holiday feeling was there and she was so happy to go to California!

21 When Mrs Germaine came back from the restroom, they finally went in the direction of the counter where they could register their luggage. "Oh no, the next queue! Why are we always taking the cheapest airline, George?!", Mrs Germaine complained. "Please, Sarah, stop lamenting. This won't help us now! Next time you are going to book our tickets", Mr Germaine replied. The whole family stood at the back of the queue, waiting. Julie began imagining where the people in this line would fly to … the Maledives, South Africa or India?

22 It is incredible what you can find at an airport: doctors, pharmacies, all kinds of shops for outdoor equipment, souvenirs or underwear, little rooms for smokers, hotels … and little chapels or mosques. Julie was amazed by the variety of offers! Julie would love to have a closer look at the mosque but today her family is quite in a hurry and they don't pass it. That's why you have to go on searching the next place.

23 Right after the passenger and hand luggage check there was the last "check point". "This will be the last line and the last check, I promise", Peter said. At the end of this line there was a police officer checking the passports of all the passengers. Since Julie was still a teenager, she was allowed to go to the police officer together with her mum. The man scanned their passports, looked closely at Julie and her mum and let them pass afterwards. "Wow, they are checking everything in detail which is good, I don't want to have any criminals in my plane", Julie thought.

24 You cannot only find a mosque but, of course, also a Christian church at Heathrow airport. The Germaines are not very religious but like going to the church for Christmas or Easter. Julie imagines that there are often people travelling or staying at the airport during Christmas or Easter time, so for them it must be practical to have a church there. Today, they are in a hurry and need to rush to their gate, so there is no time to visit the church. Go on searching the gate.

My reading trail:

1											

Vocabulary

mosque	Moschee	**equipment**	Ausrüstung
security guidelines	Sicherheitsrichtlinien	**hand luggage**	Handgepäck
to annoy	stören	**announcement**	Durchsage
ticklish	kitzelig	**access**	Zugang
charger	Ladegerät	**mess**	Schweinerei, Unordnung
rom-com	(romantische) Liebeskomödie	**to lament**	lamentieren, sich beklagen

At the airport
Lesespurgeschichte (2)

Julie and her family planned to fly to San Francisco in the summer holidays and do a road trip in California by renting a camper van. It was her first transatlantic flight and that's why she was extremely nervous and did not know what to expect. Her older brother Peter had already been to the US with their uncle, so he was an expert when it came to longer flights.

If you want to know what Julie experienced at the airport, start reading at number 1.

1 The Germaine family had two large suitcases and a smaller one, which they planned to take into the cabin as hand luggage. Julie had to share a suitcase with her mother because her parents told her that they would take the subway from the airport to the hotel in San Francisco. Afterwards they also had to walk about 15 minutes, so she was not allowed to take too much stuff with her for the time in California. As the suitcases were heavy, Julie's uncle drove the family to the airport by car. They arrived at the entrance of the airport and uncle Jim dropped them there.

2 After some long minutes the queue had finally diminished and it was their turn. Julie's parents showed all the four passports to the lady who was wearing an elegant costume with the logo of the airline on it. In Julie's eyes she looked very important. The lady started typing their data into her computer and printed the boarding passes for the four of them. "Oh we don't need them", Mr Germaine said. "I have all the boarding passes in the wallet on my phone. I think this is quite useful because we are saving paper. We are green eco-friendly people, you know?" "George, stop telling the woman our whole life story. Take the boarding passes, they are useful because we can give them to Julie and Peter. In case they get lost, they will know where to go, people can help them find us or they can even board the plane without us."

If you want to know how many hours the Germaine family has to fly to get from London to San Francisco, solve the following riddle:

Number of inhabitants of the city of London: .... **million +**

Number of airports in the greater area of London: .... **airports –**

Number of seasons every year has: .... **seasons**

.... + ... – .... = ...

You will also know where you have to go on reading.

3 This is the gate where the plane to Singapore is going to board soon. Julie's parents had always wanted to fly to Singapore but with the high humidity and extreme heat there in August they decided to fly to California instead. They were sure that San Francisco and the national parks would be an exciting experience for Julie and her brother which they would totally enjoy. But one day, they will definitely go to Singapore to have a look at the amazing Marina Bay Sands and the Gardens by the Bay. So this is not the correct gate, go back to the last place and search the right one.

4 This is not the correct entrance for the hand luggage check and the passenger screening. This is the entrance for business and first class passengers. Julie's dad had checked the prices for a business class ticket because he had taken business class flights when he was in the US for work and in his opinion, it was really comfortable. In the economy class he always had problems to fit into the seat because his legs are so long! But the prices were high, so they could not afford it for the whole family, not even for Mr Germaine. In the end, they decided that it's not worth to spend so much money on a plane ticket but that it makes more sense to use it for activities in California with the whole family. So that's why they don't use this entrance today, please go back to the last place.

5 After Peter got his hot dog, the family continued their way through the airport building. "Peter, be careful!! You are making a mess with your ketchup! See, you've spilled some of it on our new suitcase!" – "Ah, come on, don't exaggerate! At least, we will recognise the suitcase on the baggage carousel hahaha! You probably don't know that but there are always so many suitcases or bags which look the same and it gets difficult to find yours. A friend of mine even took the wrong suitcase home lately which he only realised at home because he opened it and found clothes that did not belong to him! Can you believe it?" "Peter, stop talking, we need to move on! But first I'll need a toilet", Mrs Germaine shouted. So the whole family moved in the direction of the toilets.

6 This is not the correct room. This is the lounge where the business class passengers can eat something before their flight. Julie saw expensive looking bottles and tables with nice decoration and fresh flowers. Obviously, the people had the opportunity to eat something and have a nice drink before boarding the plane. Some people also use the lounge to sit at the desks and continue working. "One day, I'll also be able to get into this comfortable lounge before I go on a business trip", she dreamed. Today she has to go on finding the gate for her flight and sit on a bench with all the other people flying economy class, so please go to the next place.

7 Of course, it's always like that! Julie knew it! As soon as they enter the airport building, Peter shouts: "Muuuuum, daaaaad, I'm hungry, I need something to eat!" "Oh no, Peter, why are you ALWAYS hungry? That's incredible", Julie replied. "My dear little sister, I am two years older than you are, plus I am 20 cm taller than you AND I am still growing. Over there is a bakery, I'll get myself a hot dog. That's perfect to get in the right mood for our stay in the US."

8 When you come to the airport there are many different counters of many different airlines. Air Austria, Delta, United, Quantas … just to name a few of the well-known ones. Some airlines cooperate and build a group so you can collect miles when flying with all of them. If you collect enough miles, you can buy something with them or enter the business lounge before a flight. Some people, who collected a lot of miles, can even upgrade their flight to business class. Unfortunately, this is not the correct desk to drop off the luggage of the Germaine family. This is the counter of SunExpress, an airline only offering flights in Europe and not to the US. Please look for the correct airline and go back to the last place.

9 At this food stall you can only buy fast food: burgers, fries, grilled cheese sandwiches. No, Julie is not allowed to eat so much fast food! Only from time to time her mum makes an exception when they are on a long trip in the car for example but usually this is not the case. And wow, this food is also pretty expensive! That's incredible. The prices are about one third higher than in the city centre, Julie realised. "Probably that's normal at the airport", she thought. Julie wanted to have some yoghurt with fruits or a salad. So please find the correct spot where Julie can get healthier food and go back to the last place.

10 When they found out that their flight to San Francisco would be leaving from gate C27 the Germaines went to the control point where all the passengers were checked and screened along with the hand luggage. Again, the next line. "When you go to an airport, you have to stand in line a lot", Julie thought. Even though this began to annoy her, she tried her best to stay positive since she didn't want to fall in a bad mood. She wanted to keep on looking forward to her great trip to sunny California! Julie was very ticklish and had to laugh when the lady screened her with the stick. At the same time, she felt safer because of this detailed control.

11 Julie held her boarding pass in her hands and was so happy! She was so much looking forward to this trip and the long flight. She had heard that there are small screens at the back of each seat so that everybody can watch their own film during the flight. What kind of films would they have this time? She hoped that she could see the latest romantic comedy which had just premiered a few weeks ago. Now the whole family was standing in front of the huge sign indicating the departure times and the gates for all the flights around the world. And everybody was searching their flight BA287 to San Francisco.

An IATA airport code is a three-character code designating many airports around the world. The airport in Paris, which was named after the former president Charles de Gaulle, has the code "CDG", for example.

Now, you have to guess! Which cities are referred to with the following codes?

– BKK: ....

– DXB: ....

– SFO: ....

– VIE: ....

– LAX: ....

– LHR: ....

12 This is a shop where you can buy all sorts of electronic devices: headphones, mobile phones, chargers, portable loudspeakers … That's a paradise for Peter and Julie's mum because they are totally into technology and fascinated by shops like this! When the family passes such a shop, It's always difficult for Mr Germaine to prevent them from spending lots of money for things they already possess but still want the newest and most modern version. Mr Germaine thinks the old equipment should be used until it doesn't work anymore. Today he is lucky, his wife and his son don't even see the shop.

13 In front of this gate Julie sees two football teams, a female and a male one both wearing their team jerseys. Where are they going? Against which team will they be playing there? Both teams were very loud and suddenly started to cheer when their plane was ready to board. Honestly, Julie was happy that the teams were not on her plane. She prefers to have a quiet flight so she can watch interesting films. As this is not the correct gate of Julie's flight, please continue searching the next place.

14 After the passport check the four of them walked in the direction of their gate which was next to a big shelf with newspapers from all over the world. Mr Germaine started looking at them picking a French and a German newspaper for the long flight. "Oh noooooo", Mrs Germaine sighed, "we are at the wrong gate, they changed it. Let's get up and hurry up, we need to get to a different part of the building." How stressful … they started running and overtaking people who were slowly strolling around without being in a rush. Peter bumped into a young lady who nearly dropped her coffee-to-go cup. "Soooooorrry", he shouted quickly and they all continued their way.

15 Of course. In front of the ladies' toilet there was a long queue! Whereas Peter and Mr Germaine quickly walked into the men's toilet and left it after a short while, Mrs Germaine had to wait for minutes. She was already getting nervous because it was quite urgent. In the meantime, Julie was keeping an eye on the family's luggage while looking at a small kiosk with books and newspapers. She was proud that her parents trusted her with this job of guarding the luggage. She bought a crime novel for the flight since she didn't know if she would like the films on board of the airplane.

16 When the Germaine family finally arrived at the correct gate, they were all out of breath and stressed but relieved having made it in time. They sat down and started waiting, Julie read her novel and Peter checked messages on his phone. Just seconds later, the employees of the airline made an announcement explaining that boarding would be done in different groups. At the beginning first and business class passengers and families travelling with young children under the age of 6 were allowed to board the plane. "They do it like this to avoid chaos on board and that not everybody rushes inside at the same time", Peter explained. Julie was annoyed by her older brother being such a know-it-all and just looked at her ticket realising that they were group two meaning they would soon be allowed to enter the plane as well.

17 This is a little food stall only selling coffee: cappuccino, espresso, latte … and obviously there were a lot of tired people at the airport because there was a loooooong queue. Many people standing in line there were wearing suits or business dresses and looked like they were travelling for work. "Business trips must be exhausting", Julie thought. She was sure that for a few weeks it would be interesting but after that it would get exhausting. She prefers travelling for private reasons. Besides, she doesn't drink coffee yet and hence doesn't start queuing here.

Flights are usually numbered based on their direction of travel.
To the left of a flight number there is a two-character code identifying the airline.
So if the code of their flight is "BA287", the name of the airline they are taking is

B .... **A** ....

18 In front of you is the entrance for the train to terminal 2. Since the airport of London Heathrow is huge, there is more than one terminal and some airlines only operate from the other terminals. So passengers sometimes have to take the little train to transfer to the other building of the airport. Julie thought it would be fun to take this train but today they already arrived at the correct terminal (probably uncle Jim had checked it before) and don't need it. Hopefully next time! This means you have to go back to the last place.

19 Some gates do not have a direct access to the plane, but you need to take another bus which takes you to your plane. Every year there are more and more people flying around the world and that's why the airports sometimes don't have the capacity to park all the planes right in front of the building. Some wait a little further away. Last year when Julie flew to Spain, she had to take such a bus because their plane was parked a few minutes away. Today they don't need to take a bus but their plane has direct access to the building. That's why this is not the correct place.

20 Inside the plane, when they put their small suitcase in the shelf above their heads and stowed the rucksack underneath the seat in front of them, they all started relaxing finally. This morning at the airport had been more stressful than expected! The stewards explained the security guidelines, showed everyone how to use the life vests and how to fasten the seatbelts. Julie checked the board entertainment system and was super happy realising that her beloved rom-com was part of the film offer. Now, finally the holiday feeling was there and she was full of anticipation to go to California!

21 When Mrs Germaine came back from the restroom, they finally went in the direction of the counter where they could register their luggage. "Oh no, the next queue! There are so many people standing in line. Why are we always taking the cheapest airline, George?!", Mrs Germaine complained. "Please, Sarah, stop lamenting. This won't help us now! Next time you are going to book our tickets and everything will be better", Mr Germaine replied. The whole family stood at the back of the queue and started to wait. Julie began imagining where the people in this line would fly to … the Maledives, South Africa or India?

22 It is incredible what you can find at an airport: doctors, pharmacies, all kinds of shops for outdoor equipment, souvenirs or underwear, little rooms for smokers, hotels ... and little chapels or mosques. Julie was amazed by the variety of offers! The mosque at Heathrow airport even offers services twice a day in different languages. Julie would love to have a closer look at it but today her family is quite in a hurry and they don't pass the mosque. That's why you have to go on searching the next place.

23 Right after the passenger and hand luggage check there was the last "check point". "This will be the last line and the last check, I promise", Peter said and pretended to be an expert. At the end of this line there was a police officer checking the passports of all the passengers. Since Julie was still a teenager, she was allowed to go to the police officer together with her mum. The man scanned their passports, looked closely at Julie and her mum and let them pass afterwards. "Wow, they are checking everything in detail which is good, I don't want to have any criminals in my plane", Julie thought.

24 You cannot only find a mosque but, of course, also a Christian church at Heathrow airport. The Germaines are not very religious but like going to the church for Christmas or Easter. Julie imagines that there are often people travelling or staying at the airport during Christmas or Easter time, so for them it must be practical to have a church there because like this they can also go to mass during this important time. Today, they are in a hurry and need to rush to their gate so there is no time to visit the church. Go on searching the gate.

My reading trail:	1											

At the airport
Lösungen

My reading trail:	1	7	5	15	21	2	11	10	23	14	16	20

Solutions:

Riddle to **2**: Number of inhabitants of the city of London: **9** million +
Number of airports in the greater area of London: **6** airports –
Number of seasons every year has: **4** seasons = **9** + **6** – **4** = **11 (11th flight from London to San Francisco)**.

Riddle to **11**: BKK: Bangkok, DXB: Dubai, SFO: San Francisco, VIE: Vienna (Wien), LAX: Los Angeles, LHR: London

Riddle to **17**: Flights are usually numbered based on their direction of travel. To the left of a flight number there is a two-character code identifying the airline. So if the code of their flight is "BA287", the name of the airline they are taking is **British Airways**.

Saving the environment: a "Fridays for Future" demonstration
Lesespurlandkarte

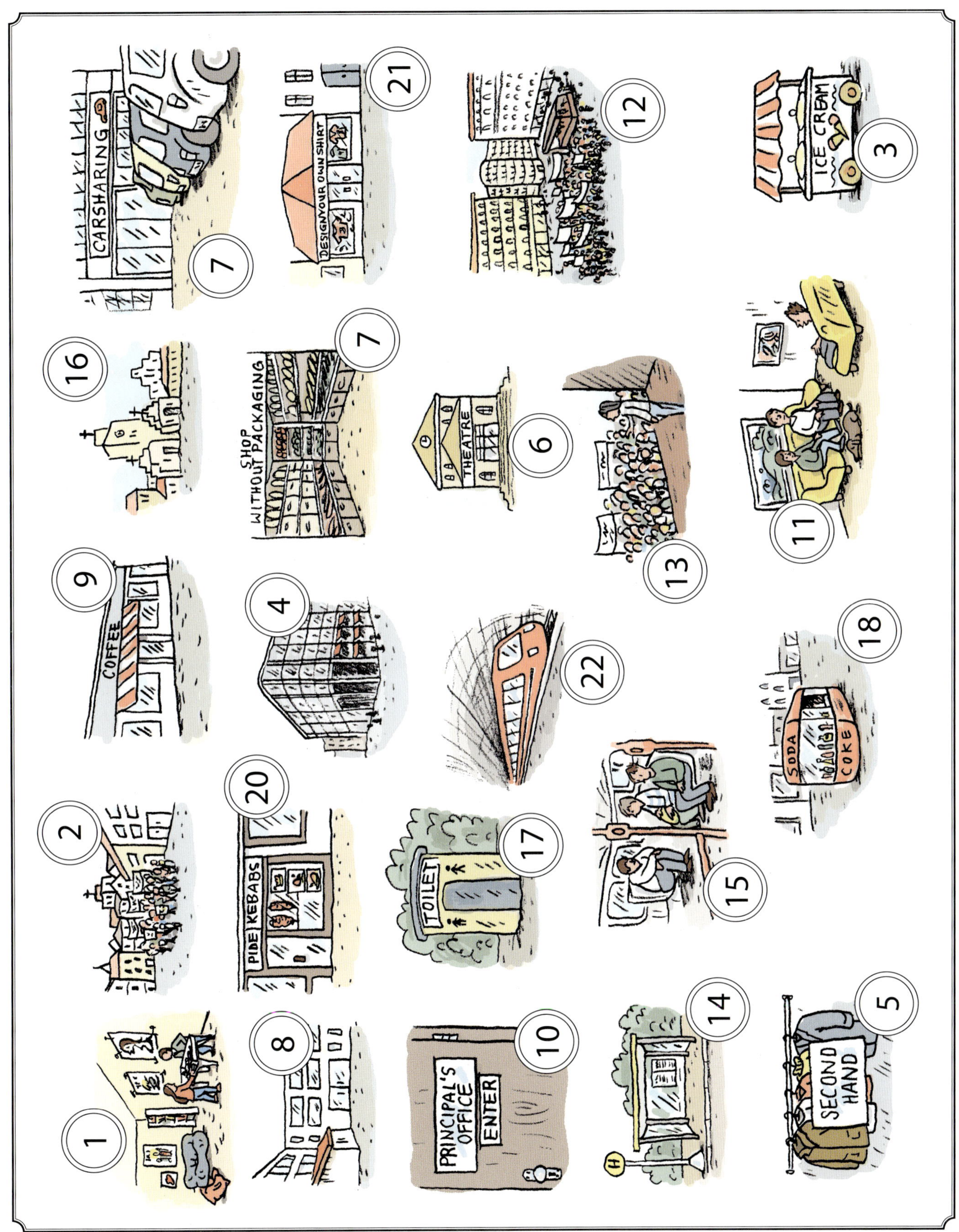

Saving the environment: a "Fridays for Future" demonstration
Lesespurgeschichte (1)

Probably you've heard of it: students skip school on Fridays to go to demonstrations! Yes, it's Fridays for Future! In advance, many students design posters, write demands to politicians on their t-shirts and create slogans they can shout during the demonstration. Usually, the students meet at 12 o'clock **i**$_{11}$n the morning in front of the station and walk around the city until arriving at the town hall. Today, Jennifer, John and Leo also want to be part of such a demonstration for the first time.

If you want to know more about their first FFF demonstration, start reading at number 1.

1 Before they leave to the station, they meet in the student's room of their schoo**l**$_{2}$ to get their posters, put on their shirts and prepare for the demonstration. The students' room is a little room on the ground floor of the school building. It is fully furnished. There are sofas to hang out, shelves with books and the highlight: a table football! "I'm so excited to be there myself", Jennifer says. "Yes, we are part of something BIG! There will be FFF demonstrations everywhere around the world today. Students are powerful!", Leo adds.

2 You probably know that wh**e**$_{7}$never people are fighting for something, there are others who do not share their opinion or their vision and believe in something else. Some believe the gouvernment should rather invest money in the country's economy or big companies because they can offer jobs. As everybody knows that FFF demonstrations take place on Fridays, a counterdemonstration was announced and people with other posters and slogans are also in town. Here at the market square the counterdemonstration meets. Of course, our three friends don't go here. Go back and search the correct meeting point.

3 The three friends go back home after the demonstration and are happy! "This will definitely not be my last FFF demonstration. It was great and it feels so good to be part of this movement with all the other young people from our town!", Jennifer says. On their way back to the train station, they pass by a little ice cream shop and get themselves some ice cream after this exciting but also stressful day.

4 "Thanks, man, buying these drinks was a really good idea. It's so warm, we need water", Jennifer says. The three friends walk with other people from their school, some of them are older, some are younger, but they all believe that it is important to stop the climate change! As the crowd is huge, they don't move that qu**i**$_{3}$ckly, stopping from time to time. They first stop in front of a huge department store where the friends see a lot of interested people looking at them.

5 In front of you is a second-hand shop. There you can buy clothes that have been wo**r**$_{10}$n by somebody else before, so you kind of recycle them which is good for the environment. Jennifer recently decided that she doesn't want to buy her clothes in shops with products from countries where children have to work or where adults work under inhumane conditions. Today, she doesn't have time to look at the newest clothes in the second-hand shop because the crowd continues their way, so please go on searching the next stop.

6 The second stop after the depar**t**$_{6}$ment store is in front of the theatre in the city centre. At each stop more young people join the crowd so it gets bigger and bigger. Before the demonstration you find information on the internet about the route of the protest march. So Jennifer, John and Leo know that they will also pass by their school after the theatre but they are sure that no teachers or other classmates will see them because the crowd is so huge. But still, John is nervous.

7 Close to their favourite Turkish restaurant, there is another new shop in the neighbourhood. It's the office of a car sharing company! Car sharing is also a very good way of avoiding pollution since people are sharing cars by renting them for a certain time instead of buying their own car. If you own a car, you use it way more often because people are generally lazy! Today, John and his friends don't go close to this place because their demonstration starts in the city **c**$_{1}$entre and not where their school and the Turkish restaurant are located.

8 On the way out of the school building John suddenly hesitates. He is not sure if he should join the demonstration. "Guys, you know that our headmaster said we would have to bring an official letter of excuse from our parents to explain why we didn't attend classes today or the day will appear as unexcused in our reports. I have many important plans for next year, I am thinking about my internship in the airline industry." "John", Jennifer replies. "Don't hesitate. I see your point, but I think you will be happy after going there, it's for an important mission. Besides, I am sure you will be able to do your internship nevertheless."

9 In one corner of the Central Square there is a little café which sells the best cake ever, namely John's favourite: cheesecake! They have a recipe with a long fa**m**$_{4}$ily tradition. Even though the group of demonstrators passes by the café they don't have time to sit down and enjoy a piece of cake. Next time!

10 This is the office of Mr Lewis, the headmaster of their school, where s**t**$_{9}$udents go if they want to talk about an important topic or if they didn't follow the rules. John is afraid that he has to go there after the demonstration but he heard from older students that Mr Lewis is rather tolerant and even thinks of them as a good idea! This means, nobody has to go to his office today, so please go on searching the next place.

11 When John arrives at home after finishing the ice cream, he tells his parents about this special day. When he is about to finish his talk, his mother suddenly asks: "Wait, John, your timetable says that you had physics in period 5 and chemistry in period 6. How come you left school so early?" "Yes, mum, I am sorry, we didn't go to these classes because we went to the demonstration. I know that was not okay but I'll make up for everything that I missed today! I just think it's so important!" "Well, I am not happy that you missed classes and I definitely don't want you to do that every week. But if it happens from time to time and you promise to make up for everything, then It's okay for me. I share your opinion that young people should raise their voices!" John is relieved and happy at the same time – this was a perfect day!

12 Of course, nothing happens when they pass the school building and so they soon come to the final destination which is the Central Square in the city centre. One of the leading girls of the group organised a meeting with politicians on a stage where demonstrators can ask questions. John is excited which politicians they will meet, he has some important questions to ask! When they arrive and see the politicians on stage, John is brave enough to go on stage and ask two of his questions. He is proud afterwards because his questions were provocative and the politicians had a hard time finding a good answer.

13 Next to the stage where the young people can ask their questions there is a second stage. When the politicians leave, everybody realises that something else is going on there and some of the representatives of the group prepare to give a speech and talk to the crowd. John is impressed by the way especially one young girl talks to the others. "What an inspiring girl", he thinks and is happy about being here instead of sitting in the physics lesson. THIS is more important!

14 Close to the school there are several bus stops because students come from different parts of the city and they have to take different buses to go back home. This is not the correct stop where the bus to the city centre leaves. From here, they can only go to the train station in the south of the city where trains to the south of the country leave. Today they don't need to go here. Go back to the last place.

15 They leave the school building and ta**k**$_{12}$e the bus to the city centre. Jennifer and Leo manage to convince John that he should join them and he agrees to do so finally. In the bus they meet some other classmates who had the same idea and also want to take part in the demonstration. They sit together in the back of the bus and because they are not the only ones who go to the event John feels better. He is hoping that his parent**s**$_{8}$ will understand and write this letter of excuse for him.

16 Here you've arrived at the Church Square in the city centre where the old Anglican church is. On Sundays you can see lots of people going to the service wearing elegant clothes. The speaker of the counterdemonstration puts up his speaking table here to talk to the people attending this second demonstration. Go back to the last place because Jennifer, John and Leo don't want to listen to him.

17 This is the public toilet in the city centre. The mayor even set up more toilets last year because of the regular FFF demonstrations. He thinks especially young people should not have to pay for going to the restroom. Today, John, Jennifer and Leo don't even have time to think about a toilet as they are walking with the crowd. So they don't need the toilet today which means you have to go back to the last place.

18 John agrees to what Jennifer said. He would not feel good about appearing on TV and his parents don't know what he is doing. "It's pretty warm today, I think I need something to drink before we start marching around the city centre screaming the whole day", John adds and leaves to go to the kiosk next to the train station. Over there, he buys three bottles of soda and two vanilla cokes for Jennifer and himself. Now they are prepared to start the tour around the city. Sugar is important when it's hot!

19 The crowd of young people passes by a small shop selling things without packaging. This is a new trend because you avoid wasting plastic. These shops usually sell food like pasta, lentils, oats, nuts but also useful things for your daily life like soap, washing powder or cleaning equipment. Unfortunately, today Jennifer and John don't have time to enter the shop, so go on searching the next place.

20 Not f**a**$_{5}$r from school, there is a little Turkish restaurant selling food like kebab where our three friends often buy their lunch. The food in the cafeteria is obviously another problem, because it is way too unhealthy and sugary. Sadly, today the restaurant is closed, so they can't have lunch there.

21 Here is the shop where you can bring a shirt and they print whatever you want on it. So Leo, Jennifer and John brought their shirts there and had their slogans printed on them. When Leo picked them up he was happy with the results. Th**e**$_{13}$y only paid 10 pounds per person which is a good price! Today, they are well prepared and don't need to go there again, so please continue your way to the next stop.

22 When they arrive at the main station, the three teenagers see lots of people holding up posters. The atmosphere is special and Leo has the feeling he is part of something big and important. "Guys, I am so happy we decided to come here. Look, over there, there is even a TV team interviewing young people." "That looks interesting but we are not in school, so I wouldn't like to be on TV right now", Jennifer says.

My reading trail:

1										

Solution word: The Fridays For Future demonstrations are part of the Global Youth .... It began in the years 2018 and 2019 and became very famous after the 2019 "Global Week for Future" which was a series of 4500 strikes across over 150 countries mainly on Friday the 20th September and Friday the 27th September.

Vocabulary

to skip school	die Schule schwänzen	**recently**	kürzlich
furnished	möbliert	**to hesitate**	zögern
restroom	Toilette, WC	**to convince**	überzeugen
counterdemonstration	Gegendemonstration	**to waste**	verschwenden
convenient	praktisch	**to contain**	enthalten

Saving the environment: a “Fridays for Future” demonstration
Lesespurgeschichte (2)

Probably you’ve heard of it: students skip school on Fridays to go to demonstrations! Yes, it’s Fridays for Future! In advance, many students design posters, write demands to politicians on their t-shirts and create slogans they can shout during the demonstration. Usually, the students meet at 12 o’clock **i**$_{11}$n the morning in front of the station and walk around the city until arriving at the town hall. Today, Jennifer, John and Leo also want to be part of such a demonstration for the first time.

If you want to know more about their first FFF demonstration, start reading at number 1.

1 Before leaving to the station, they meet in the student’s room of their schoo**l**$_{2}$ to get their posters, put on their shirts and prepare for the demonstration. The students’ room is a little room on the ground floor of the school building which was designed and furnished by the students themselves. There are sofas to hang out, shelves with books and the highlight: a table football! Some children also come here to do their homework or receive extra help in some subjects from older students. “I’m so excited to see the Fridays for Future demonstrations myself”, Jennifer says proudly. “Yes, we are part of something BIG! There will be FFF demonstrations everywhere around the world today. Students are powerful!”, Leo agrees.

2 You probably know that wh**e**$_{7}$never people are fighting for something, there are also others who do not share their opinion or their vision and believe in something else. Thinking of climate change, there are also people who believe the gouvernment should rather invest money in the country’s economy or in big companies offering jobs to people. As everybody knows that the FFF demonstrations take place on Fridays, a counterdemonstration was announced and people with other posters and slogans are also marching around town. Here at the market square the counterdemonstration meets. Our three friends don’t identify with it and that’s why they don’t go here. Go back and search the correct meeting point.

What else can you do to save or protect the environment? Think of some ideas!

➞ ………………………………………………………………

➞ ………………………………………………………………

➞ ………………………………………………………………

➞ ………………………………………………………………

3 Joyful and fulfilled, the three friends go back home after the demonstration! “This will definitely not be my last FFF demonstration. It was great and it feels so good to be part of this movement with all the other young people from our town!”, Jennifer says. On their way back to the train station, they pass by a little ice cream shop and get themselves some ice cream as a reward after this exciting but stressful and exhausting day. Jennifer talks to the owner of the Italian ice cream shop and tells them about the demonstration. The man is very interested and didn’t know that the FFF demonstrations are also taking place in this city!

4 “Thanks, man, buying these drinks was a really good idea. It’s such a warm day that we need water”, Jennifer says as they start walking in the huge crowd of people. The three friends walk with other people from their school, some of them are older, some are younger, but they all have one thing in common: their fight for the environment of our earth. As the crowd of people is so huge they don’t move that qu**i**$_{3}$ckly, stopping from time to time. They first stop in front of a huge department store where the friends see a lot of interested people looking at them.

5 In front of you is a second-hand shop. You can buy clothes there which have been wo**r**$_{10}$n by somebody else before, so you kind of recycle them by wearing them. For families with a lot of children, this is a convenient and cheaper way to buy clothes and for the environment It’s also good. Jennifer recently decided to

………………………………………………………………

be more careful where she buys her clothes. She heard a presentation about the problems of "fast fashion" in her politics class and learned that she quite often bought clothes in shops with products from countries where children have to work or adults work under inhumane conditions without being paid appropriately. "This is something I don't want to support", she agreed to herself! Today, she doesn't have time for the second-hand shop because the crowd moves on, so please go on searching the next stop.

6 The second stop after the depar**t**$_{6}$ment store is in front of the theatre in the city centre. At each stop more young people join the crowd so it gets bigger and bigger. Everybody is wearing t-shirts and holding posters with catchy slogans so that town politicians would finally feel the need to do something about climate change! Before the demonstration you find information on the internet about the route of the protest march. So Jennifer, John and Leo know that they will also pass by their school after the theatre but they are sure that no teachers or other classmates will see them because the crowd is so huge. But still, John is nervous and even thinks about walking with his head bend down when they pass the school.

7 Close to their favourite Turkish restaurant, there is another new shop in the neighbourhood. It's the office of a car sharing company! This is also a very good way of avoiding pollution since people are sharing cars by renting them for a certain period of time instead of buying their own car. If you own a car, you tend to use it way more often because people are generally lazy! John's mother has recently rented a car there and was very happy with the system, the nice people working there and the service in general. She agreed to use car sharing again instead of buying a second car for the family. Today, John and his friends don't go there because their demonstration starts in the city **c**$_{1}$entre and not where their school and the Turkish restaurant are located.

8 On the way out of the school building John suddenly hesitates. He is not sure if he should join the demonstration. "Guys, you know that our headmaster said we would have to bring an official letter of excuse from our parents to explain why we didn't attend classes today or the day will appear as unexcused in our reports. I have so many important goals for next year, I am thinking about my internship in the airline industry." "John", Jennifer replies. "Don't hesitate. I see your point, but I certainly think you won't regret going there as you will be fighting for an important mission. Besides, I am sure you will be able to do your internship nevertheless." "I heard about so many students from other schools and other classes who have already gone to such a demonstration and nobody was in trouble. I am sure it won't be a problem for your internship, it will rather be an advantage because the company will see that you are active and care about our world", Leo adds.

9 In one corner of the Central Square there is a little café which sells the best cake ever, namely John's favourite: cheesecake! They have a recipe which has a long fa**m**$_{4}$ily tradition. Whenever he goes there to eat the delicious cake, John almost tastes the love with which they bake this amazing cake. They offer cheesecakes in many different styles: with blueberries or strawberries on top, with a chocolate flavour, with roasted almonds on top Even though the group of demonstrators passes by the café they don't have time to sit down and enjoy a piece of cake. Next time!

Think of a catchy slogan for a poster that you could take to a FFF demonstration.

....

....

10 This is the office of Mr Lewis, the headmaster of their school, where s**t**$_{9}$udents sometimes go if they want to talk about an important topic or if they didn't follow the rules. John is afraid that he would end up there after skipping school but he heard from older students that Mr Lewis is rather tolerant regarding the FFF demonstrations. He secretly has the opinion that young people should show the older politicians that they have to take actions before the situation gets even worse! He also told his teachers recently to talk more about the problems of climate change during their lessons. This means, nobody has to go to his office today, so please go on searching the next place.

11 When John arrives at home after finishing the ice cream, he sits down in the living room with his parents and tells them everything about this special day. When he is about to finish his talk, his mother suddenly asks: "Wait, John, your timetable says that you had physics in period 5 and chemistry in period 6, how come you left school so early? Were the teachers ill today?" "No, mum, I am sorry, we skipped these classes to attend the demonstration. I know that was not okay but I'll make up for everything that I missed today, I promise! I just think it's so important to do something about climate change and that's why I went to the demonstration." "Well, I am not happy that you missed classes and I definitely don't want you to do that every week but if it happens from time to time and you promise to make up for everything, then it's okay for me. I share your opinion, it's necessary that young people start raising their voices. They are powerful!" John is relieved and happy at the same time – this was a perfect day!

12 Of course, nothing happens when they pass the school building and so they are soon about to reach the final destination of the demonstrators which is the Central Square in the city centre. One of the leading girls of the group organised a meeting with politicians on a stage where all the young people can attend and ask questions. John is excited which politicians they will meet because he has important questions to ask! When they arrive and see the politicians on stage, John is even so brave to go on stage and ask two of his questions. "Sir, how can you justify that our local senate has recently spent millions of pounds to build a new parking garage although our school wanted to be more ecological and build a waste separating system and the mayor declined the idea claiming that there was not enough money for projects like this?" He is proud afterwards because his questions were provocative and the politicians had a hard time finding a good answer.

13 Next to the stage where the young people can ask their questions there is a second stage. When the politicians leave, everybody realises that something else is going on there and some of the representatives of the group prepare to give a speech and talk to the crowd. John is impressed by the way especially one young girl talks to the others. "What an inspiring girl, such a role model", he thinks and is definitely happy about being here instead of sitting in the physics lesson. THIS is more important!

14 Close to the school there are several bus stops because students come from different parts of the city and have to take different buses to go back home. John and Jennifer go by bike every morning, but Leo has to take a bus. Taking the bike is not an option for him because then he would have to get up at 6 a.m. every morning – way too early. This is not the correct stop where the bus to the city centre leaves. From here, they can only go to the train station in the south of the city where the trains to the south of the country leave. Leo has once taken this train when he visited his aunt but today they don't need to go here. Go back to the last place.

15 They leave the school building and ta**k**$_{12}$e the bus to the city centre. Jennifer and Leo manage to convince John that he should join them and he agrees to do so. The argument that "he would be part of something bigger" convinces him. In the bus they meet some other classmates who had the same idea and also want to take part in the demonstration. They sit together in the back of the bus and due to the fact that they are not the only ones joining the event John feels better. He is just hoping that his parent**s**$_{8}$ will understand and write this letter of excuse for him but this is something he will start worrying about later.

16 Here you've arrived at the Church Square in the city centre where the old Anglican church is located. On Sundays you can see lots of people going to the service wearing elegant clothes. Today the speaker of the counterdemonstration puts up his speaking table here to talk to the people attending this second demonstration. These people do not share the same values like our three friends. They believe that the young people demonstrating against the climate change are exaggerating. You have to go back to the last place because Jennifer, John and Leo don't want to listen to this speaker on Church Square.

17 This is the public toilet in the city centre. The mayor even set up more toilets last year because of the regular FFF demonstrations. He thinks especially young people should not have to pay for going to the restroom. Today, although they drank so much because of the heat, John, Jennifer and Leo don't have time to think about a toilet as they are walking with the crowd cheering their slogans. So they don't need the toilet today which means you have to go back to the last place.

18 John agrees to what Jennifer said. He would not feel good about appearing on TV and also his parents don't know what he is doing. "It's extremely warm today, I think I need something to drink before we start marching around the city centre screaming the whole day", John adds and leaves to go to the kiosk next to the train station. Over there, he buys three bottles of soda and two vanilla cokes for Jennifer and himself because he knows that Leo wouldn't like such a sweet drink. Now they are prepared to start the tour around the city. Sugar is important when it's hot, so the circulation won't collapse. He also thinks about buying something to eat but they will do so later.

19 The crowd of young people passes by a small shop selling things without packaging. This is a new trend because you avoid wasting plastic. These shops usually sell food like pasta, lentils, oats, nuts but also useful things for your daily life like soap, washing powder or cleaning equipment. Jennifer and John have already seen it when they went shopping in the city centre two weeks ago. They agree to come back soon to buy something there. Unfortunately, today they are in the middle of the crowd and don't have time to enter the shop, so please go on searching the next place.

20 Not f**a**$_{5}$r from school, there is a little Turkish restaurant selling food like pide or kebab where our three friends often buy lunch when they don't like the cafeteria food. This is obviously another problem, they agree on discussing it with the headmaster one day because it is way too unhealthy. Of course, crisps, chocolate and muffins are delicious, but contain too much sugar and fat which should not be consumed on a regular basis by teenagers who are still growing. John and Leo became friends with the son of the owner of the Turkish restaurant and now they come more often. Sadly, today the restaurant is closed, so they can't have lunch there.

21 Here you see the shop where you can bring a shirt and they print whatever you want on it. So Leo, Jennifer and John brought their shirts there two weeks ago (when they started planning their participation in the FFF demonstration) and showed the man behind the counter their slogans and pictures. They discussed the design of their shirts and the man promised to finish printing the shirts just in time for the demonstration. Two days later, Leo picked up the shirts and was happy with the results, also because it was not that expensive. Th**e**$_{13}$y only paid 10 pounds per person which is an appropriate price! Today, they are well prepared and don't need to go there again, so please continue your way to the next stop.

22 Arriving at the main station, the three teenagers can see lots of people holding up posters with spicy slogans. "Make the planet GRETA again", "There is no plan(et) B" or "We need action" are just a few examples! Everybody is chatting and the atmosphere is special. Leo, in particular, has the feeling he is part of something big, a huge movement. He knows about the importance of young people uniting to set a sign against global warming. "Guys, I am so happy we decided to come here. Look, over there is a TV team interviewing young people." "That looks interesting but we are skipping school right now so I wouldn't have a good feeling to be on TV. What if my mum sees me … she doesn't know about me being here", Jennifer says.

A very famous climate activist from Sweden is G .... T ....

In January 2021, she turned .... years old. If you find out her age, you will also know where you have to go on reading.

My reading trail:	1										

Solution word: The Fridays For Future demonstrations are part of the Global Youth .... It began in the years 2018 and 2019 and became very famous after the 2019 "Global Week for Future" which was a series of 4500 strikes across over 150 countries mainly on Friday the 20th September and Friday the 27th September.

Saving the environment: a "Fridays for Future" demonstration
Lösungen

My reading trail:	1	8	15	22	18	4	6	12	13	3	11

Solution word: **climate strike**

Solutions:

Riddle to **2**: What else can you do to save or protect the environment? Think of some ideas!
eat less meat, try to use less plastic, wear second-hand clothes, take your bike or a bus to go somewhere (instead of going by car), avoid trips by plane, recycle everything you can, buy local food

Riddle to **9**: individual answers

Riddle to **22**: A very famous climate activist from Sweden is **Greta Thunberg**. In January 2021, she turned **18** years old.

At Notting Hill Carnival
Lesespurlandkarte

At Notting Hill Carnival
Lesespurgeschichte (1)

Last year, Sarah and her class had planned to go to Notting Hill Carnival but they could not go because the Carnival parade did not take place for several reasons. This is why she was looking forward to join this event that she had seen on TV a few times but never had the chance to go.

If you want to know how Sarah and her classmates experienced this special day, start reading at number 1.

1 Sarah lives in a small town outside of London and going to the city centre takes about 50 minutes. But she is not allowed to go alone. Today she goes with her class and two teachers. They met in Kingston at the station to take the train to King's Cross and from there another one to Notting Hill Gate. In the train were a lot of people and Sarah could not find a place to sit. Her best friend Lisa found a seat and Sarah stood next to her so they could chat about the latest school gossip.

2 While Sarah was standing on the pavement watching the dancers performing, she started to worry a bit. What if she didn't have an internet connection for google maps to find her way back to the phone shop? She checked her phone: no connection. Suddenly she felt someone touching her from behind trying to tickle her. "What the h …", she turned around surprised when she realised it was Noah again. This time she was even happy to see him – they could start searching the phone shop together now. "That's it! I know what to do. Maybe one of the restaurants or shops in this area has open WIFI, then we load the way to the google maps app and find our group!", Sarah said.

3 At King's Cross Station, the whole class 7E got out of the train and stood on the platform. Mrs Campbell stood on a bench and said: "Please listen to me, everybody! We are now at King's Cross Station and we have to take another train to Notting Hall Gate, the Victoria Line westbound. Please stay close to the group and don't get lost! London is a huge and also a dangerous city and I don't want to search you everywhere or go to the police."

4 When they arrived at Notting Hill Gate, they got out of the underground station and felt the great atmosphere in this part of the town. Woooow, there were so many smells (food stalls with Indian, Jamaican or African food), colours, sounds … Sarah was overwhelmed! She knew she would like it, but this was better! They walked a few metres and stopped next to a small shop. "THIS", said Mrs Campbell, "this is our meeting point. Whatever happens and in case you get lost you will have to try and come back here. We meet at 4 o'clock, that's when we head back home. It's the phone shop at the beginning of Aberdeen Street, everybody remember it! Phone shop in Aberdeen street."

5 In Notting Hill there are a lot of old-looking shops selling old paintings, cutlery, jewellery, furniture or dishes. Sarah's grandma loved them and when she was still alive, she took Sarah with her from time to time. Sometimes they talked to the shop owners who knew interesting stories about the objects. Afterwards, grandma always invited Sarah to have a cup of hot chocolate at her favourite café. Walking around these shops reminded Sarah of the lovely afternoons with her grandma and she was just grateful for the memories. Sadly, today she didn't have time for a shop visit because she had to continue her search for her friends.

6 "Okay, that's important, I have to remember it … phone shop in Aberdeen street", Sarah repeated. After a few minutes of walking with the whole group, they stopped at a crossing where Notting Hill Street meets Kensington Park Road and Mrs Campbell talked to them again. "So here we are, this is the start of the street parade. Mrs Fletcher and I decided that you will be allowed to walk around in groups of three in this area. You have my telephone number and if anything happens, you get lost or anything, please call me. I am here to help you if there's a problem. But let's hope everything will be fine. Enjoy the parade and the great costumes and have some nice food. See you at the phone shop. Have fun!"

7 That was nice of Mrs Campbell to allow the students to walk around on their own. Sarah knew that this was proof for Mrs Campbells trust in them. Sarah liked Mrs Campbell so much, other teachers would not have allowed that. So Sarah decided to go with Lisa, of course, and her other good friend Anna. "Oh my God, girls, look at all the food stalls", Lisa shouted. "Let's get some Indian curry, or better, an African mixed plate, it smells delicious!" "Yeah, the food looks amazing, but I'll have fish and chips for starters and then a more exciting dessert. You can get your African plate here and I'll be back in a minute with fish and chips", said Sarah. "Yeah, sure, good plan", Lisa answered.

8 Where are the girls? Mh, Sarah decided to wait a few minutes. She finished her food and then went to the toilet area to see if she could find the girls somewhere. Afterwards, she decided that the best way to make use of this day was to watch the Carnival parade. "I am here for the first time in my life, so I will enjoy it, even alone. No reason to panic!", she said to herself. She went back to the street and watched the parade with all the dancers in shining costumes with huge jewellery and make-up. A group of men was throwing fire torches in the air!

9 People from a lot of different countries live in London. You find their influences at Notting Hill Carnival as well: there are so many food stalls from different countries. Here you are in front of a food stall selling German food like pretzels, sausages and beer. Apart from the fact that Sarah is too young to drink beer, she doesn't find German food appealing, so please continue searching the next place.

10 Sarah was lost in her thoughts when the underground arrived. The two teachers took care that everybody got in and nobody was left on the platform. Inside the train, Sarah suddenly had to go to the toilet. "Oh no", she thought, "not now!" Next to her was her classmate Noah who had just decided to play a trick on her: he started to tickle her and Sarah had to laugh so hard her whole body was shaking. She could not escape Noah's attack because the train was so full, but she was moving and started to bump into other people. "Noah, please stop, I am annoying other people." "It's okay, don't worry. I'll stop. I had enough fun looking at you like this", Noah replied.

11 This is another platform at King's Cross Station where you can take a different line. London is a huge city with several underground lines, like for example the Picadilly Line, Circle Line or Bakerloo Line. Underground lines work differently in different cities and countries but the one in London is not so difficult to understand for tourists. This is the wrong platform. From here, no trains leave for Notting Hill, they only go to the east of the city. Please go on searching the next stop.

12 You are in front of a stall where little children can get funny make-ups. There is a nice-looking lady painting a butterfly, a tiger or a zebra on their faces. Sarah liked doing something like this when she was a little girl but now she was too old for that. Besides, there are many more interesting things to do at Notting Hill Carnival so she doesn't have time for this. So you have to go to the next place.

13 Right now you are next to another shop close to Notting Hill Gate but it's not the phone shop in Aberdeen Street where Sarah and her classmates were supposed to meet their teachers before going back home to Kingston. It is a very colourful shop selling Carnival costumes like pilots, nurses, ET and different animals like tigers, cats or frogs. She only had time for window-shopping but had to hurry and look for her friends, so please go back to the last place.

14 "Hello, young lady, what a beautiful day today, isn't it?", the old man of the fish-and-chips shop welcomed her. "Oh yes, it is, I am enjoying the Carnival", Sarah replied. "I'd like to have some fish and chips, please." "Okay, there you go, enjoy!" And because it's your first time here, I'll give a bit of my special Notting Hill Carnival sauce extra to try it! "Thank you." Sarah tried the fish and chips, they were good, and the sauce … oh my, it was so delicious! She turned around and went back to the African food stall. When she arrived, she couldn't find Lisa and Anna.

15 This is the big stage where singers and bands perform their songs during the Carnival time. The performers speak different languages, some of them wear traditional costumes. The group of dancers from Brazil are usually the best. They come from Rio de Janeiro, a city well-known for its Carnival culture. The Brazilian dancers always wear colourful costumes with feathers, glitter and veeeery short clothes. Sadly, the stage is too far away from Sarah, she decided to watch it on TV later at home and not to go there. Otherwise it would be even more difficult to find the way back to the meeting point with her teachers.

16 In front of you there is a group of teenagers close to a red telephone booth. Sarah didn't know any of them, it must be some class from another school. When they got out of the underground at the beginning, she had already realised that several other classes from different schools in London had had the same idea: to go to Notting Hill Carnival as well. So this must be the meeting point of another group. You have to go on searching the phone shop where Sarah's class meets.

17 When Carnival season starts, nearly all shops, restaurants or cafés decorate their windows with colourful decoration, feathers or balloons! Here you are in front of a vet surgery selling dog and cat food as well. Even this vet decorated his window. Sarah has a cat at home, so she also needs a vet from time to time but today she didn't have time for the decoration, the street parade was more interesting and besides she really needed to find the phone shop in Aberdeen Street. So please go back to the last place!

18 After 40 minutes Sarah moved through the passengers to talk to her teacher, Mrs Campbell. She teaches literature – not Sarah's favourite subject, she is more into science and maths. "Mrs Campbell, where exactly are we getting off the train? And how long does it take us to go there?" "Oh hi Sarah, I hope you are fine. We still need another five to ten minutes and we will be getting off at King's Cross, so please pay attention and don't miss the stop where we will leave the train. And Sarah, dear, you could pass this information on to your classmates", her teacher answered.

19 This is the little café where Sarah used to go with her grandma. It's a cute café with a lot of old objects hanging on the wall: old paintings, small sculptures, a compass, little figures made from wood. The owner is also very nice: Mrs McGregor from Scotland with a Glasgow accent. Sarah and her grandma kept coming back because they had the best hot chocolate in town and from time to time Sarah was allowed to add marshmallows. So yummy! From the street with the antique shops you had to walk about ten minutes to get to the café so it's too far away and Sarah can't make it. Go on searching the next spot!

20 When walking around Notting Hill, Sarah immediately had to think of the famous film "Notting Hill" with Julia Roberts and Hugh Grant – a great film. Sarah also would have loved to have a look at the book shop from the film but she didn't know where to find it. But she would come back in the next weeks for that! Maybe she could ask her mum if she wanted to join her because she also liked the film a lot. So that's a plan for next time, now please go on searching the next place.

21 After Mrs Campbell's little speech they left and went down to the underground platforms, always focused on staying close to the group. When they arrived, the platform was crowded. They had to wait for five minutes which is quite a long time in London where the trains sometimes come within a minute during rush hour in the early evening. "Please mind the gap." Sarah had to smile. This announcement is typical for London's underground and the speaker has been the same for ages.

22 That's what they did! Luckily, they found an open WIFI at a coffee place and found the way back. When they arrived at the phone shop everybody was relieved: they had already been waiting for Noah and Sarah. Especially Lisa, Anna and Noah's two friends were glad their friends didn't get lost. They were already worried. What an exciting day this trip to Notting Hill Carnival has been! Nevertheless, Sarah enjoyed it a lot and planned to come back next year. Maybe, after this episode, her parents will allow her to go to the city centre of London on her own. She has shown that she knows how to solve a difficult situation!

My reading trail: | 1 | | | | | | | | | | | |

Vocabulary

to tickle	kitzeln	**crossing**	Kreuzung
nurse	Krankenschwester	**surgery**	Praxis
latest	der, die, das Jüngste, Neueste, Letzte	**speech**	Rede
cutlery	Besteck	**to be glad**	froh sein
to solve	lösen	**appealing**	ansprechend
pavement	Bürgersteig	**relieved**	erleichtert

At Notting Hill Carnival
Lesespurgeschichte (2)

Last year, Sarah and her class had already planned to go to Notting Hill Carnival but when the time came they could not go because the Carnival parade did not take place for several reasons. That was why she was so much looking forward to this event that she had already seen on TV a few times but never had the chance to join.

If you want to know how Sarah and her classmates experienced this special day, start reading at number 1.

1 Sarah lives in a small town in the suburbs of London and going to the city centre takes her about 50 minutes. She sometimes goes there with her parents and her sister but until now she has not been allowed to do so alone because her mum is worried that unknown people might talk to her or bother her otherwise. Today she is with two teachers and her whole class, so everything is fine. They met in Kingston at the station to take the train to King's Cross and from there another one to Notting Hill Gate. The train was already pretty crowded and Sarah did not find a place to sit because there was an elderly lady to whom she offered her seat. Good girl! Her best friend Lisa found a seat and Sarah just stood next to her so they could chat about the latest school gossip (Who wrote the best mark in the last history test? Who will be our new PE teacher next year? Do you already know the new girl in the other class?).

2 While Sarah was standing on the pavement watching the dancers and jugglers performing she started worrying a bit. What if she could not find her way back to the phone shop? What if she didn't have internet connection to use google maps to find her way? She checked her phone and she was right: no connection (probably there were too many people in this area). "Don't panic, you will be fine", she was telling herself when she suddenly felt someone touching her from behind trying to tickle her. "What the h…", she turned around surprised when she realised it was Noah again. This time she was even happy to see him as they could start searching the phone shop together now. "That's it! I know what to do, let me check if one of the restaurants or shops in this area has open WIFI, then we load the way to the google maps app and follow it. Once it's loaded you don't need internet connection. We will find the way back to our group!", Sarah said.

3 At King's Cross Station, the whole class 7E got out of the train and stood on the platform. Mrs Campbell stood on a bench so that everybody could see her as she was about to explain where they would have to go next. "Please listen to me, everybody! We are now at King's Cross Station and have to take another train to get to Notting Hall Gate. This will be the Victoria Line westbound. Please stay close to the group and focus on not getting lost! London is a huge and also dangerous city and I don't want to be forced to search you everywhere or go to the police."

4 When they arrived at Notting Hill Gate, they got out of the underground station and could already feel a spark of the great atmosphere in this part of the town during Carnival season. Woooow, so many smells (food stalls with Indian, Jamaican or African food), colours, sounds … Sarah was overwhelmed! She knew she would like it, but she had not imagined it to be so amazing and exciting! They walked a few metres and stopped next to a small shop selling credit for phone calls and SIM cards for all over the whole world. "THIS", said Mrs Campbell while pointing at the shop, "this is our meeting point. Whatever happens and in case you get lost you will have to try and come back here. We meet here, at the latest at 4 o'clock because then we have to head back home. It's the phone shop at the beginning of Aberdeen Street, everybody please remember it! Phone shop in Aberdeen street."

Do you know other cities around the world where Carnival is very famous?

....

5 In Notting Hill there are a lot of antique shops selling old paintings, cutlery, jewellery, furniture or dishes. Sarah's grandma loved shops like this and when she was still alive, she took Sarah with her from time to time.

....

Luckily, she never bought anything because she always said that she didn't need so many things anymore but she liked looking at the items and chatting to the owners of the shops. Sometimes they told them interesting stories about the objects on display, where they came from and who used to own them. Afterwards, grandma always invited Sarah to a cup of hot chocolate at her favourite café. Strolling past the antique shops reminded Sarah of those lovely afternoons with her grandma and she was grateful to have these memories. Sadly, today she didn't have time for a shop visit because she had to continue her search for her friends.

6 "Okay, that's important, I have to remember it … phone shop in Aberdeen street", Sarah repeated a few times to remember it correctly. London is a huge city and you never know what might happen. After a few minutes of walking with the whole group, they stopped at a crossing where Notting Hill Street meets Kensington Park Road and Mrs Campbell talked to them again. "So here we are, this is the start of the street parade. Mrs Fletcher and I decided that you will be allowed to walk around in groups of three (that's the absolute minimum) in this area. You have my telephone number and if anything happens, you get lost or anything, please don't hesitate to call me. I am here to assist you in an emergency. But let's hope everything will be fine, enjoy the parade and the great costumes and have some nice food. See you at the phone shop. Have fun!"

7 That was nice of Mrs Campbell to allow the students to walk around on their own. Sarah knew that this was proof for Mrs Campbells trust in them: that they would know how to help themselves and how to behave in an emergency. This was one of the reasons why she liked Mrs Campbell so much, other teachers would not have allowed that. So Sarah decided to go with Lisa, of course, and her other good friend Anna. "Oh my God, girls, look at all the food stalls", Lisa shouted. "Let's get some Indian curry! Oh no, wait, I'd rather go for an African mixed plate with lentils and veggies, it smells delicious!" "Yeah, you're right, the food looks amazing, but I think I'd prefer fish and chips for starters and then a more exciting dessert. You can get your African plate here and I'll be back in a minute and get some fish and chips over there", said Sarah. "Yeah, sure, good plan", Lisa answered.

8 Where are the girls? Mh, Sarah decided to wait a few minutes, maybe they went to the toilet? She finished her food and then went to the toilet area (she had seen it on the way) to see if she could find the girls there. Afterwards, even though she was not successful, she decided that the best way to make use of this day was to watch the Carnival parade, nevertheless. "I am here for the first time in my life, so I will enjoy it, even alone. No reason to panic!", she said to herself. So far, so good. She went back to the street and stood on the pavement to watch the parade with all the dancers in colourful, shining costumes with huge jewellery and make-up. There was even a group of men juggling fire torches! Stunning!

9 London is a multicultural city: people from a lot of different countries live here. These cultural influences are visible in various places of the city. It's not only the restaurants, you also see it in clothes or book shops. Here, at Notting Hill Carnival, there are many food stalls from different countries, that makes it difficult to decide which one you want to try. Especially when you are not good at making decisions, just like Sarah! Here you are in front of a food stall selling German food like pretzels, sausages and beer. Apart from the fact that Sarah is too young to drink beer, German food doesn't look very appealing to her, so please continue searching the next place.

10 Sarah was lost in her thoughts when the underground arrived and they all tried to get inside. That was not easy: the arriving train was already quite packed. But they managed since their two teachers took care that everybody got in and nobody was left on the platform. Inside the full train, Sarah suddenly felt the need to go to the toilet. "Oh no", she thought, "not now!" The classmate next to her, Noah, had just decided to play a trick on her. Suddenly, he started to tickle her and Sarah had to laugh with her whole body shaking. She could not flee and escape Noah's attack because the train was so packed, but she was moving and started to bump into other people. "Noah, please stop, I am annoying other people." "It's okay, don't worry. I'll stop. I had enough fun looking at you like this", Noah replied. "Thank God", Sarah thought.

11 This is another platform at King's Cross Station where you can take a different line. London is a huge city with several underground lines, like for example the Picadilly Line, Circle Line or Bakerloo Line. There is a colourful map indicating the different stops of each line for people who are not familiar with London's underground system, so they don't get lost. Underground lines work differently in different cities and countries but the one in London is not so difficult to understand for newcomers. Unfortunately, you are at the wrong platform here. From here, no trains leave for Notting Hill, they only go to the east of the city. Please go on searching the next stop.

12 You are in front of a stall where little children can get funny make-ups. There is a nice-looking lady painting a butterfly, a tiger or a zebra on their faces. Sarah liked doing something like this when she was a little girl but now she feels too old to do it again – even though it's a nice thing to preserve a part of your childhood while growing up. ☺ Besides, there are many more interesting things to do at Notting Hill Carnival so she doesn't have time for this. Go on searching for the next place.

13 Right now you are next to another shop close to Notting Hill Gate but it's not the phone shop in Aberdeen Street where Sarah and her classmates were supposed to meet their teachers before going back home to Kingston. It is a very colourful shop selling Carnival costumes and showing them on display in the shop window. Apparently, you can buy the costumes of a pilot, a nurse, ET and different animals like tigers, cats or frogs. Sarah was happy they did not sell costumes for different nationalities, to look like a person from China or India. She found these costumes inappropriate and even a bit racist. She liked the window-shopping but could not go inside because she had to hurry and search her friends, so please go back to the last place.

14 "Hello, young lady, what a beautiful day today, isn't it?", the old man of the fish-and-chips shop welcomed her. "Oh yes, it is, I am enjoying the Carnival, it's my first time here", Sarah replied. "That's great, I hope you are having a wonderful and exciting day. What can I get you?" "I'd like to have some fish and chips, please." "Okay, there you go, enjoy! And because it's your first time here, I'll give a bit of my special Notting Hill Carnival sauce extra to try it!" "Thank you so much, that's very kind of you." Sarah tried the fish and chips, they were good, but the sauce … oh my, it was so delicious! Probably the best sauce she had ever had with fries. She was still amazed when she turned around and went back to the African food stall. She arrived and realised that Lisa and Anna were nowhere to be found.

Do research on the internet and find three films that take place in Notting Hill.

➡ ....

➡ ....

➡ ....

15 This is the big stage where singers and bands perform their songs during the Carnival time. Here you also see multicultural London: the performers speak different languages, some of them wear traditional costumes. The most impressive performance is usually the one by the dancers from Brazil. They are from Rio de Janeiro, a city well-known for its Carnival culture. The Brazilian dancers always wear huge and colourful costumes with feathers, glitter and veeeery short clothes. Sadly, the stage where the musicians perform is too far away from Sarah, that's why she decided to watch it on TV later at home and not to go there. Otherwise it would be even more difficult to find the way back to the meeting point with her teachers.

16 In front of you there is a group of teenagers close to a red telephone booth. Sarah didn't recognise any of the faces, so it must be some class from another school. When they got out of the underground at the beginning, she had already realised that several other classes from different schools in London had had the same idea: to go to Notting Hill Carnival as well. So this must be the meeting point of another group. This means you have to go on searching the phone shop where Sarah's class meets.

17 When Carnival season starts, nearly all shops, restaurants or cafés decorate their windows with colourful decoration, banners, feathers or balloons! Here you are in front of a vet surgery selling dog and cat food as well. Even this vet decorated his window for this special time of the year. He doesn't decorate his window for Christmas or Easter with so much passion! Sarah has a cat at home, so she also needs a vet from time to time but today she didn't have time to look at the shop window and the decoration, the street parade was more interesting and besides she really needed to find the phone shop in Aberdeen Street. So please go back to the last place!

18 After 40 minutes Sarah moved through the passengers to talk to her teacher, Mrs Campbell. If they didn't have Mr Johnson as their new chemistry teacher, Mrs Campbell would be Sarah's favourite. Nevertheless she likes her a lot because she often plans trips with her class and is a very nice and caring person. She teaches literature which is not Sarah's favourite subject, she is more into science and maths. "Mrs Campbell, where exactly are we getting off the train? And how long does it take us to go there?" "Oh hi Sarah, I didn't see you coming. I hope you are fine. We still need another five to ten minutes and we will be getting off at King's Cross, so please pay attention to the announcement and don't miss the station where we will leave the train. And Sarah, dear, you could pass this information on to your classmates, just as a short reminder", her teacher answered.

19 This is the little café where Sarah used to go with her grandma. It's a cute café with a lot of antique objects hanging on the wall: old paintings, small sculptures, a compass, little figures made from wood or pewter. The owner is also very nice: Mrs McGregor from Scotland with a heavy accent from Glasgow. Sarah and her grandma kept coming back because they were offering the best hot chocolate in town and from time to time Sarah was allowed to add marshmallows. So yummy! From the street with the antique shops you had to walk about ten minutes to get to the café so it's too far away and Sarah can't make it today. Go on searching the next spot!

20 When walking around Notting Hill, Sarah immediately had to think of the famous film "Notting Hill" with Julia Roberts and Hugh Grant – a great film! Parts of it take place in a tiny book shop in Notting Hill. A lot of tourists come to this part of the town every year to have a look at the book shop and imagine the famous film scenes. Sarah also would have loved to see the book shop but she didn't know where to find it and didn't have internet connection to find out the exact location. But she would come back in the next weeks to search the book shop and browse through the books on offer. Maybe she could ask her mum if she wanted to join her because Sarah remembered she also liked the film a lot. So that's a plan for next time, now please go on searching the next place.

21 After Mrs Campbell's little speech they left and went down to the underground platforms, always focused on staying close to the group, as their teacher had said earlier. When they arrived, the platform was quite crowded. No wonder, at 9 o'clock in the morning a lot of people are busy on their way to work and in London the only convenient way to get there quickly and in time is the underground – the traffic is crazy. They had to wait for five minutes which is quite a long time in London where the trains sometimes come within a minute during rush hour in the early evening. "Please mind the gap." Sarah had to smile. This announcement always reminds her of London's underground and the speaker has been the same for ages. "Have they ever recorded it with a new speaker?", she wondered.

22 That's what they did! Luckily, they found an open WIFI at a coffee place and managed to find the way back. When they arrived at the phone shop everybody was relieved: they had already been waiting for Noah and Sarah. Especially Lisa, Anna and Noah's two friends were glad their friends didn't get lost. They were already worried. What an exciting day this trip to Notting Hill Carnival has been! Nevertheless, Sarah enjoyed it a lot and planned to come back again next year. Maybe, after this episode, her parents will allow her to go to the city centre of London on her own. She has proven that she knows how to solve a difficult situation!

My reading trail:	1											

At Notting Hill Carnival
Lösungen

My reading trail:	1	18	3	21	10	4	6	7	14	8	2	22

Solutions:

Riddle to **4**: Carnival is also very famous in Cologne (Germany) or Rio de Janeiro (Brazil).

Riddle to **14**: Other films that take place in Notting Hill: Performance (1970), Lava (2001), Paddington (2014)

An internship at a hotel
Lesespurlandkarte

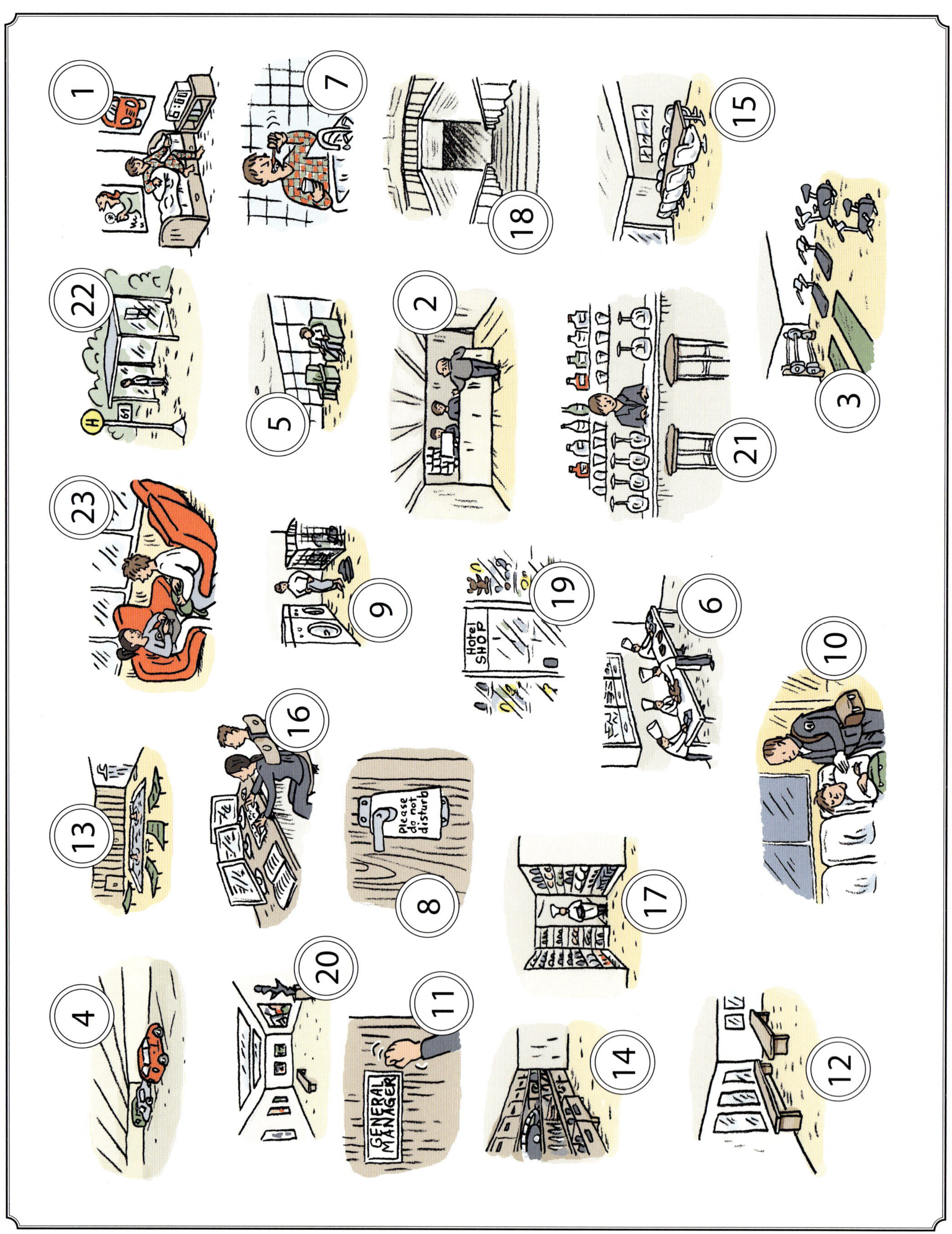

An internship at a hotel
Lesespurgeschichte (1)

In year 8 all the students at Jackson Pollock High School in Virginia have to do an internship to get an idea about the job they want to choose later in life. The whole topic was not easy for Jeff. He did not know AT ALL what was suitable for him and what he wanted to do. Luckily one of his teachers showed them how to write an application letter for an internship, otherwise this would have been a first difficulty. In the end, he decided to apply for an internship at a hotel.

If you want to know whether Jeff liked his internship and how he experienced the first day at the hotel, start reading at number 1.

1 For the internship Jeff had an online interview with a nice lady working at the hotel. She explained everything he needed to know. The lady asked why Jeff had chosen a hotel for his internship and he said that he liked travelling with his family during the holidays and always liked the special hotel atmosphere. He also could make use of his foreign-language skills. So the lady told him to arrive at 8 a.m. on the first day. Jeff woke up early at 6 a.m., better be on time!

2 A good introduction is very important for every job, so Jeff followed her to the front desk of the reception and listened. While Mrs Laurence was explaining something to him, an old man approa**c**$_{4}$hed them at the counter and started to talk. He didn't notice that he interrupted a conversation. "The person in the room next to me is a snorer and the coffee at the breakfast buffet was not hot enough this morning …", he complained. "Excuse me, Sir, would you give us a minute to finish, then we will be happy to help you", Jeff said. After two minutes, he wrote down the complaints and passed the note to an employee who promised to see to it. Mrs Laurence was proud of him because he stayed calm even though this older man was a difficult guest.

3 In this room the guests of the hotel find fitness equipment: two weight benches, some bikes, a few steppers and so on. This place is busy in the morning and in the evening when the hotel guests finish their program of the day. Jeff likes sports, but he prefers outdoor sports like biking, climbing or playing football. He thinks that these fitness centres are a good invention for people on business trips. Jeff has some more tasks today, so please go on searching the next place.

4 You entered the car park of the hotel where guests may leave their cars during the stay. They have to pay ten dollars a day which is a good price. Jeff generally does not understand why some people always go everywhere by car even though they could take the bus or the train. Obviously this is not the place where Jeff continues the second part of his first day at the hotel, so please try to find the correct location.

5 When he arrived, he told the man at the reception who he was and that his internship started today. "Oh alright, you're Jeff. Welcome! Could you please sit in one of these armchairs in the lobby and wait until Mrs Laurence comes to pick you up? She will show you around and explain everything to you." So Jeff sat down in an armc**h**$_{5}$air and looked at the different people passing by: old people, young people, businessmen, tourists with cameras … He looked at an older couple and tried to listen to them. What language were they speaking? Jeff decided to ask them in the next days.

6 After meeting the Colombian couple, it was time for Jeff's lunch break but – he had forgotten his lunch box at home in the fridge. Oh no! Maybe he could ask in the kitchen if they had something for him? In the kitchen he talked to Josh, the very nice chef, and got a yummy sandwich! "No worries, Jeff, if this happens again, just come over and we'll find something for you. Nobody has to be hungry here! But I am sorry we have a lot of work to do, I need to continue now."

7 "Honey, do you want to have breakfast?", his mum shouted from downstairs. "No, no, I am fine, thank you", Jeff answered. He was not hungry but nervous. An internship was definitely different from going to school and he felt like an adult doing something important in life. Jeff showered, brushed his teeth and then put on the good new clothes he had bought with his mum for the internship. About ten minutes later he was on the way to take the bus to the city centre.

8 "Please do not come in" – Oh, Jeff didn't see the sign at the door of this room. There are personal things on the floor like clothes, shoes, a toothbrush and it looks like somebody has left this room in a hurry. Jeff remembered that Mrs Laur**e**$_{6}$nce had said at the beginning that it is very important to respect the guest's privacy. So please get out of this room quickly and go on searching the next place because this is a room where nobody should enter.

9 He was still thinking about this old couple when someone shouted: "Oh hey, Jeff, nice to see you! Did you find our place without problems? How are you doing? Are you excited about the first day? Are you excited about the first day? Looking forward to the internship?" Oh wow, so many questions, let's hope she slows down a bit. "Sorry, I always ask too many questions at the same time. Don't worry, when I start explaining how everything works, I will not talk so quickly!", Mrs Laurence added. "Thank you so much for the nice welcome", Jeff said to Mrs La**u**$_{3}$rence. "Let's get started. You need clothes for the internship, you have to wear the shirt with our logo and the elegant trousers that everybody is wearing here. Let's go to the basement, there is the laundry and they will give you everything you need." Jeff got more excited: he would wear employee's clothes! In the basement, a nice man gave him the items.

10 Jeff missed his bus because he had talked to Tom. But he lives in a big city, so there is a bus every ten minutes. When he sat in the bus, he immediately fell asleep – what an exciting day! Jeff was happy because he had met nice people: the couple from Colombia, Tom and also Mrs Laurence was kind. Jeff missed his bus stop and rode to the final stop. The bus driver honked to wake him up. Jeff had to call his father and ask him to pick him up. Anyway, he was looking forward to the next day at the hotel! This internship was a good choice.

11 This is the room of the hotel manager. Mrs Laurence told Jeff that he works at several hotels in the city and has to go from one place to the other depending on where he has something important to do. Today nobody has seen him here. If something important has to be decided and he is not in his office, the employees can ask Mrs Laurence. Without his permission nobody is allowed to enter this office, so go on looking at the correct place.

12 At the end of the day when Jeff finished his work, he went into the staff **r**$_{7}$oom where every employee has a locker. There you can keep your personal things but also your clothes for work, then you don't have to take them home. In the staff room, Jeff met a very nice boy named Tom and the boys had a chat about the hotel. When they said goodbye they planned to meet again to play video games or football with some friends.

13 When he entered this part of the hotel Jeff could smell something nice like a shampoo. Where was he? He opened another door and realised that this must be the spa. He stood there looking at everything: there were two different saunas, a swimming pool and a massage chair. Oh, how he would love to enjoy the spa for a day! This place reminded him of a nice stay at a beautiful hotel in Austria he had once visited with his family during a skiing holiday. Well, Jeff is not allowed to use the spa, he is not here as a guest so please go back to the place where he works.

14 This room is stuffed with shower gels, shampoos, towels, toilet paper but also cleaning equipment like buckets and vacuum cleaners. Jeff has probably found the room where the housekeeping people keep all their stuff. He is not yet working with the house keeping team so he didn't need to enter this room. Please go on to the next place.

15 You are in a meeting room with many tables, a huge screen and small cabin where you can make video-calls with people from all around the world. Mrs Laurence explained to Jeff that this room is usually booked by companies. They like meetings at the place where they stay, then everybody has short ways because "time is money". If you open the door, you can see that there is a meeting right now, so please go back to the last location.

16 After Jeff changed his clothes in the bathroom, he came back to Mrs Laurence and they went into her office to sit down at a computer. She explained a few facts to him first, for example that he would get to look at all different sectors of work at the hotel. "I can tell you, room service is probably the hardest and working in the kitchen or behind the bar is also quite stressful. The most important rule when working at a hotel: the guests are king, even though they might have strange wishes sometimes. Of course, we try to make it possible so they come back. Now, I want to explain how our check-in system works but we need to go to the front desk at the reception."

17 This is the room where the kitchen staff and the chef keep the food they need to prepare breakfast and dinner. In here are a lot of shelves with boxes of jams, bread and so on, as well as some fridges with yoghurt, milk or cheese. Jeff wondered how the kitchen team manages to calculate the amount of food they need every day. This must be extremely difficult! In such a hotel kitchen, hygiene is a very important issue, so nobody is allowed to enter the room without permission. Please get out of the room and go to the next location.

18 There are several ways to move around town: the subway, the bus, taxis or bikes. Here you can take the subway to other parts of the town, you just need to go down the stairs, get a ticket and then you can enter the train. From his home, Jeff usually takes the bus, he only has to walk three minutes to the bus stop. This is not the stop for Jeff to take his bus home, go back to the last place.

19 In front of you is the little hotel shop where guests can buy souvenirs, snacks or other small things (like toothbrushes, toothpaste or even sunglasses). Mrs Laurence told Jeff that he will not be working in this shop during his internship because she thinks that he cannot learn anything there. Moreover, he lives in the same town, so he doesn't need to buy anything here. Therefore, you have to go on searching the next location.

20 In this hotel, there is also a little art gallery where local artists can show their pictures to people. If hotel guests are interested in buying one, the receptionist will give them the contact details of the artist. Jeff likes his art class in school, but he is only interested in creating something himself and not so much in looking at pictures by other people. This is why he never enters this room during his internship at the hotel. Go back to the last location.

21 After talking to the difficult guest and the introduction by Mrs Laurence, Jeff started the first part of his internship and worked at the bar. While he was trying to cut the pieces of cake correctly, the old Spanish-speaking couple came to the bar and sat down. Jeff talked to them (in Spanish, of course!) and they told him that they were from Colombia and wanted to know the way to the National Gallery, the most famous museum in town. The receptionist had told them in English which they didn't understand. Jeff managed to give them directions in Spanish! The couple was so happy with the service that they left him a tip. Jeff was very proud!

22 He stood at the bus stop waiting for bus number 61 to arrive. Suddenly he was worried. What if the guests would not take him seriously because he was so young? Would the person taking care of him be nice and explain everything so that he understands what to do? "No, stop it", he said to himself trying to push away the thoughts and be more positive and self-confident about his internship. He was lucky that the bus arrived soon.

23 He entered the bus, sat down and took **o**$_2$ut his book because he thought reading might make him a little less nervous. From the back of the bus somebody shouted: "Hey Jeff, what a coincidence! You are probably also on the way to your internship?" It was Jessica, a girl from Jeff's class. "Oh, yes, right, I am doing my internship at the Old Town Hotel in the city centre. What about you?" "Oh, sounds cool! You know I like animals, so I applied at a **v**$_1$et surgery and they accepted me! I am so excited what kind of animals will come in these two weeks. They said we might also visit 'patients' at home." "Sounds like the ideal internship for you! Let me know how it was. I have to get off the bus now. See you." Jeff got off the bus and went in the direction of the hotel which was only a five minute walk.

My reading trail:	1											

Solution word: In order to check in when arriving at the hotel, you need a ....

Vocabulary

internship	Praktikum	**self-confident**	selbstbewusst
suitable	passend	**to disturb**	stören
tip	Trinkgeld	**permission**	Erlaubnis
coincidence	Zufall	**basement**	Keller
weight bench	Hantelbank	**vet surgery**	Tierarztpraxis
staff	Belegschaft, Personal	**application letter**	Bewerbungsschreiben

An internship at a hotel
Lesespurgeschichte (2)

In year 8 all the students at Jackson Pollock High School in Virginia have to do an internship. This is very important as it provides professional experience and a first opportunity to get an idea about the job they would like to choose later in life. The whole topic was not easy for Jeff because he was a very undecided person and did not know AT ALL what kind of internship would be suitable for him and where to apply. He was lucky that one of his teachers showed them how to write an application letter. Otherwise this would have been a first difficulty for him. In the end, he decided to apply for an internship at a hotel.

If you want to know whether Jeff liked his internship and how he experienced the first day at the hotel, start reading at number 1.

1 For the internship Jeff had an interview via zoom with a nice lady from the personnel department who explained everything that he needed to know about the student internship the hotel offered. The lady wanted to know why Jeff had chosen a hotel for his internship and he replied that he liked travelling with his family during the holidays and the special hotel atmosphere. There are people talking in different languages, telling interesting stories, the different kinds of people of all ages working there … and besides he thought he might make use of his foreign-language skills obtained in school. So the lady told him to arrive at 8 a.m. on the first day to get all the things done. Jeff woke up early in the morning at 6 a.m., better be on time the first day!

2 A good introduction is very important in every job, so Jeff followed her to the front desk of the reception and listened attentively. While Jeff was still trying to master the booking system and Mrs Laurence was explaining something to him, an old man approa**c**$_{4}$hed them at the counter and started to talk without paying attention that he interrupted a conversation. "Sorry, I have to make a complaint, my door handle makes weird noises, the person in the room next to me is a snorer and the coffee at the breakfast buffet was not hot enough this morning …", he complained. "Excuse me, Sir, would you give us a minute to finish, then we will be delighted to help you", Jeff said. After two minutes, he listened to the guest's complaints again, wrote a note and passed it to the chef concierge who promised to see to it. Mrs Laurence was proud of Jeff because he had stayed calm even though this older man was obviously a difficult guest.

3 In this room the guests of the hotel find fitness equipment: two weight benches, a rowing machine, some bikes, a few steppers and so on. This place is busy mainly in the morning and in the evening when the hotel guests finish their program of the day and find time for exercising. Jeff likes sports, but he prefers outdoor sports like biking, climbing or playing football with his friends. He has never been a fan of gyms, but he thinks that these fitness centres are a good invention for people on a business trip who don't have enough time to go somewhere outside or if it's raining. Jeff has more tasks to do today, so please go on searching the next place.

4 You entered the car park of the hotel where guests may leave their cars during the stay. They have to pay ten dollars a day which is quite a good price if you compare it to the public parking garages in town. Jeff does not understand why some people go everywhere by car even though in bigger cities there is good public transportation! Haven't they heard of global warming and that cars still cause so much pollution? Unbelievable! Well, obviously this is not the place where Jeff continues the second part of his first day at the hotel, so please try to find the correct location.

5 When he arrived, he told the man at the reception who he was and that his internship started today. "Oh alright, you're Jeff, we were already waiting for you. Welcome! Could you please sit in one of these armchairs in the lobby and wait until Mrs Laurence picks you up? You already talked to her, right? She will show you around and explain everything to you." So Jeff sat down in an armc**h**$_{5}$air and waited for Mrs Laurence.

He looked at the different people passing by: old people, young people, businessmen, tourists with cameras … that was exactly what he liked about hotels, imagining where the people were from and what they were doing in the city. He looked at an older couple and tried to listen to them. He wondered what language were they speaking? Jeff decided to ask them if he got the chance to get in touch with them over the next days.

6 After this successful encounter with the Colombian couple, it was time for Jeff's lunch break but when he wanted to sit down and eat, he realised that he had forgotten his lunch box at home in the fridge. Oh no! How should he survive the rest of the day without lunch? Maybe he could ask in the kitchen if they had leftovers for him? In the kitchen he talked to Josh, the very nice chef, and he got a tasty sandwich with hummus, dried tomatoes and basil – delicious! "No worries, Jeff, if this happens again, just come over and we'll find something for you. Nobody has to be hungry here! But I am sorry we have a lot of work to do, I need to continue now."

Where would you do your internship? Write three if-clauses type II answering this question!

If I had the chance to do an internship, I would …

➡ ....

➡ ....

➡ ....

7 "Honey, do you want to have breakfast? I can make you a peanut butter jelly toast", his mum shouted from downstairs. "No, no, I am fine, thank you", Jeff answered. He did not really feel hungry and had to admit that he was even a bit nervous. An internship was definitely something different than school and he immediately felt like an adult doing something important in life. Jeff showered, brushed his teeth and put on the good new clothes he had recently bought with his mum for this purpose. About ten minutes later he was on the way to take the bus to the city centre.

8 "Please do not disturb" – Oh, Jeff didn't see the sign at the door handle of this room. Obviously, the person in here do**e**$_6$sn't want to be disturbed. There are a lot of personal things on the floor like clothes, shoes, a toothbrush, some bags and it looks like somebody has left this room in a hurry. Jeff remembered that Mrs Laurence had said at the beginning that it is very important to respect the guest's privacy and he wanted to do that. So please get out of this room quickly and go on searching the next place because this is a room where nobody should enter.

9 He was still thinking about this old couple when somebody interrupted his thoughts by shouting joyfully: "Oh hey, Jeff, nice to see you! Did you find our place without problems? How are you doing? Are you excited about the first day? Looking forward to the internship?" Oh wow, so many questions, let's hope she slows down a bit. "Sorry, I always ask too many questions at the same time, but I am curious and I like meeting new people. Don't worry, when I start explaining how everything works, I will not talk so quickly!", Mrs Laurence added. "Thank you so much for the nice welcome. I found the hotel without problems and I am actually really excited about my first day", Jeff said to Mrs La**u**$_3$rence. "Let's get started and get out of the lobby. First step is proper clothing for the internship, you have to wear the shirt with our logo and the elegant trousers that everybody is wearing here. The guests need to see who actually works here or who is just a businessman. We'll go to the basement, there we have our laundry and they also provide the clothes for our employees. Everybody gets a set of two shirts and two trousers and you have to wash them at home. As you are only 14, I think you don't need to wear a tie, that would be exaggerated." Jeff got more excited, he would wear employee's clothes! Down in the basement, they talked to a nice man who gave him everything he needed.

10 Due to the chat with Tom, Jeff missed the bus he had planned to take. But he lives in a big city, so there is a bus every ten minutes. When he sat in the bus, he immediately fell asleep – what an exciting but also stressful and exhausting day! Jeff was happy since he had met nice people: the couple from Colombia, Tom and also Mrs Laurence was a kind and good instructor. Because he had fallen asleep, Jeff missed his bus stop and rode until the final stop. The bus driver had to honk to wake him up. Oh no – Jeff had to call his father and ask him to pick him up. Nevertheless, he was looking forward to the next day at the hotel. This internship was a good choice!

11 This is the room of the hotel manager. Mrs Laurence told Jeff that he works at several hotels in the city and he always has to go from one place to the other depending on where he has something important to do. Today nobody has seen him here yet but apparently there is nothing for him to deal with. If something important has to be decided and he is not in his office, the employees can always ask Mrs Laurence, she is the deputy. Without his permission nobody is allowed to enter this office, so please go on looking at the correct place!

Show us your language skills by linking the fitting pair of sentence and language!

Dzień dobry!	**Spanish**
Hola, que tal?	**Czech**
Bom dia.	**Japanese**
Buongiorno!	**Portuguese**
Arigatō.	**Italian**
Děkuji!	**Polish**

12 At the end of the day when Jeff finished his work, he went into the staff **r**$_{7}$oom where every employee has his or her own locker. In the locker you can keep your personal belongings but also your clothes that you need to wear at work. Then you don't have to take them home, but you can come here in the morning and change before you start working. In the staff room, Jeff met a very nice boy named Tom and the boys had a chat about the hotel. When they said goodbye they planned to meet again to play video games or play football with some friends.

13 When he entered this part of the hotel Jeff could already smell something nice like a shampoo, probably Aloe vera. Where was he? He opened another door and realised that this must be the spa. Amazed by the beauty and the silence of this place he stood there and inspected everything for a while: there was a huge hot tub with steam coming out of it, two different saunas, a swimming pool and a massage armchair. Oh, how he would love to enjoy the spa for a day! This place reminded him of a nice stay at a beautiful hotel in Austria he had once visited with his family during a skiing holiday. They had always spent the time between 5 p.m. and dinner in the spa … Well, but this time Jeff is not allowed to use the spa, he is not here as a guest so go back to the place where he works.

14 This room is stuffed with shower gels, shampoos, towels, toilet paper but also cleaning equipment like cleaning rags, buckets, vacuum cleaners. Jeff has probably found the room where the house keeping people keep all their stuff. He is not yet working with the housekeeping team so didn't need to enter this room and left straight away. He remembered that many of his friends told him that they always took the little shampoos and shower gels home after staying at a hotel. Was this even allowed? Jeff didn't think so but a lot of people do that. Please go on to the next place.

15 You are in a meeting room with many tables, a huge screen and small cabin where you can make video-calls with people from all around the world. Mrs Laurence explained to Jeff that this room is usually booked by companies coming to town with a larger group of employees for important business deals. They like meetings at the place where they stay, then the employees have short ways because "time is money". If you open the door, you can see that there is a meeting right now and nobody should disturb, so please go back to the last location.

16 After Jeff changed his clothes in the bathroom, he came back to Mrs Laurence and they went into her office to sit down at a computer. She explained a few basic facts to him first, for example that he would get to look at all different sectors of work in the hotel, the kitchen/bar, the reception, the room service and the office. "I can tell you, room service is probably the hardest and working in the kitchen or behind the bar is also quite stressful. What we want to see is that you make an effort with your work, that you are willing to do this job as good as possible. The most important rule when working at a hotel: the guests are king. So we do our best we can to fulfil the wishes they have and, believe me, guests sometimes do have strange wishes. Of course, we try to make it possible, so they come back or recommend our hotel to their friends and relatives. Now, I want to explain how our check-in system works but we need to go to the front desk at the reception."

17 This is the room where the kitchen staff and the chef store the food they need to prepare breakfast and dinner. In here are a lot of shelves filled with boxes of oats, jams, bread and so on, as well as the same amount of fridges filled with yoghurt, milk or cheese. Jeff wondered how the kitchen team manages to calculate the amount of food they need every day. This must be extremely difficult! In such a hotel kitchen, hygiene is a very important issue, so nobody is allowed to enter the room without permission. Please get out of the room and go to the next location.

18 There are several ways to move around town: the subway, the bus, taxis or bikes. Here you can take the subway to go to other parts of the town, you just need to go down the stairs, get a ticket and then you can enter the train. Jeff usually takes the bus from his home because he only has to walk three minutes to the bus stop. The subway station is around twelve minutes away – of course, he is too lazy. This is not the bus stop for Jeff to take his bus home, please go back to the last place.

19 In front of you is the little hotel shop where guests can buy souvenirs, snacks or any other items they might have forgotten at home (like toothbrushes, toothpaste, liquid for contact lenses or sunglasses in summer). Mrs Laurence told Jeff that he will not be working in this shop during his internship because she thinks that he cannot learn anything there. Moreover, he lives in the same town, so he doesn't need to buy anything here. You have to go on searching the next location.

20 In this hotel, there is also a little art gallery where local artists can display their work. Here you find several pieces of art: paintings, but also sculptures, audio or video installations – created by local artists. If hotel guests are interested in purchasing a piece of art, the receptionist will give them the contact details of the artist and they can get in touch. Jeff likes his art class in school, but he is only interested in creating something himself and not so much in looking at the work of other people. This is why he never enters this room during his internship. Go back to the last location.

Hotels are international places. Do you know which flag belongs to which country?

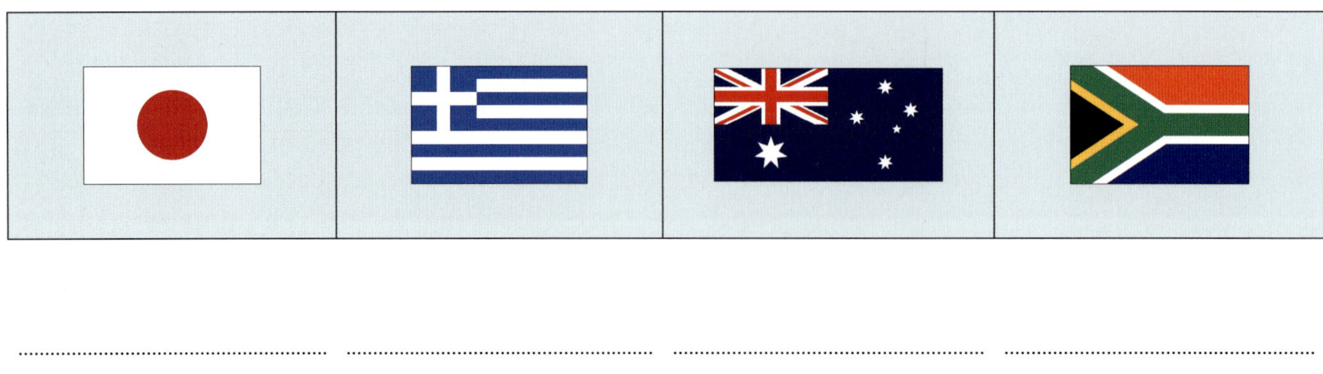

....

21 After this first encounter with the difficult guest and the introduction by Mrs Laurence, Jeff started his first part of his internship and worked at the bar. He quicky learned how to clean the glasses correctly, how to load the dish washer and how to mix the two virgin cocktails (cocktails without alcohol). While he was trying to cut the pieces of cake correctly, the old Spanish-speaking couple approached the bar and sat down. Jeff talked to them (in Spanish, of course!) and it turned out that they were from Colombia and wanted to know the way to the National Gallery, the most famous museum in town. The receptionist had told them in English which they didn't understand. In the end Jeff managed to give them directions in Spanish and the couple was so satisfied with the service that they left him a generous tip. Jeff was happy and so proud!

22 He stood at the bus stop waiting for bus number 61 to arrive, all the while wondering about his time at the hotel. What if the guests would not take him seriously because he was so young? Or even worse, what if foreign guests would not understand him? Was his Spanish good enough? Would his instructor from the staff be nice and explain everything to him so that he understands what to do? Should he maybe have chosen another type of internship? "No, stop it", he said to himself trying to push away the doubts and be more positive and self-confident about the internship. He was lucky that the bus arrived soon.

23 He entered the bus, sat down in the front part and took **o**$_2$ut his book because he thought the distraction might make him a little less nervous. From the back of the bus somebody shouted: "Hey Jeff, what a coincidence! You are probably also on the way to your internship?" It was Jessica, a girl from Jeff's class. "Oh, yes, right, I am doing my internship at the Old Town Hotel in the city centre for the entire two weeks. What about you?" "Oh, sounds cool! You know I like animals, so I decided to apply at a **v**$_1$et surgery and they accepted me! I am so excited what kind of animals will come in these two weeks. They said we might also visit 'patients' at home if their owners cannot bring them to the surgery." "Sounds like the ideal internship for you! Let me know afterwards how it was. I have to get off the bus now. See you." Jeff got off the bus and went in the direction of the hotel which was only a five minute walk.

My reading trail:

1											

Solution word: In order to check in when arriving at the hotel, you need a ....

An internship at a hotel
Lösungen

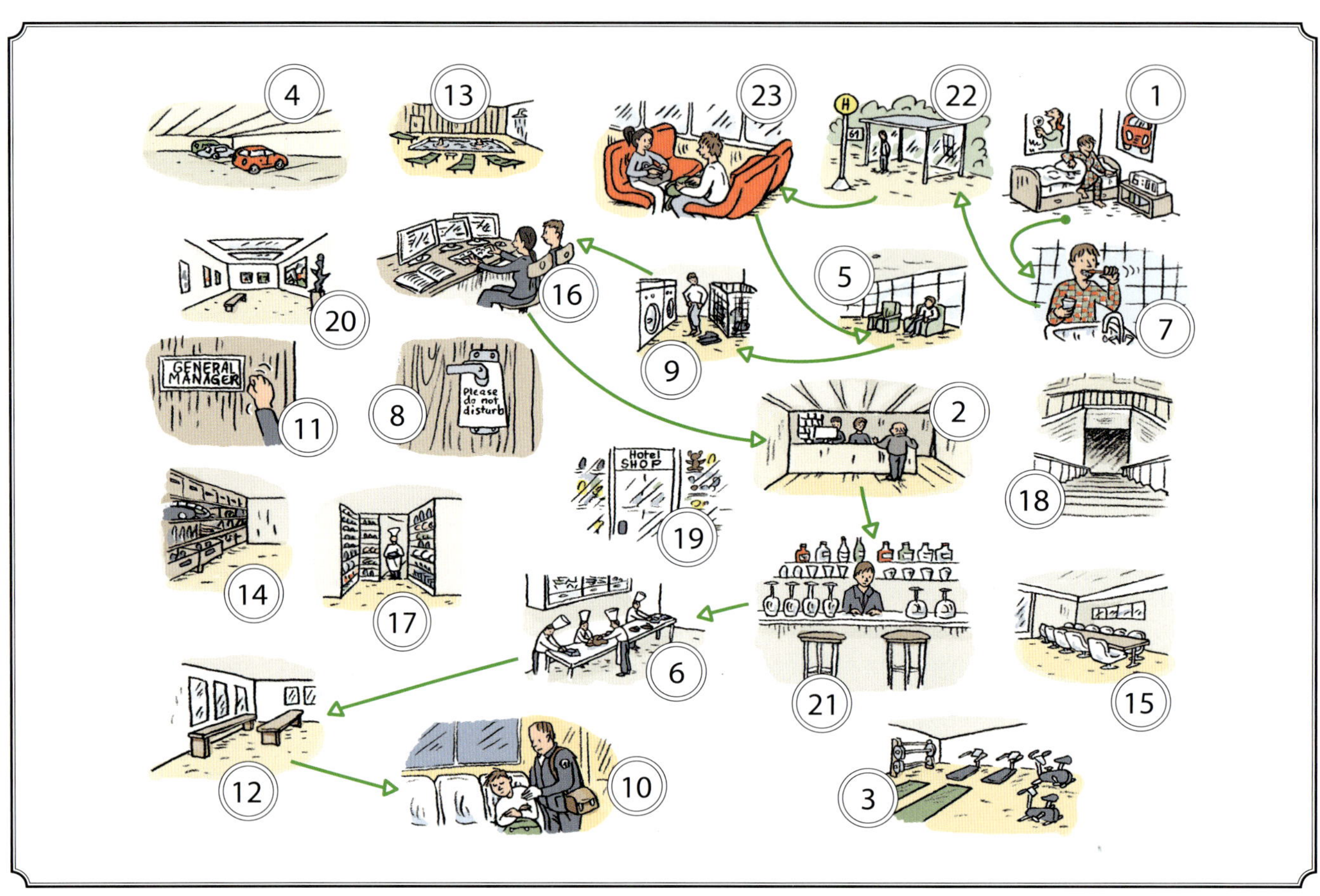

My reading trail:	1	7	22	23	5	9	16	2	21	6	12	10

Solution word: **voucher**

Solutions:

Riddle to **6**: individual answers

Riddle to **11**:
Dzień dobry! → Polish
Hola, que tal? → Spanish
Bom dia. → Portuguese
Buongiorno! → Italian
Arigatō. → Japanese
Děkuji! → Czech

Riddle to **20**: You see the flags of **Japan**, **Greece**, **Australia** and **South Africa**.

The home baking video blog
Lesespurlandkarte

The home baking video blog
Lesespurgeschichte (1)

Carrot cake, brownies, New York cheesecake ... Who doesn't like pastries, cake or cookies? Josie has always had a passion for baking and over the last months she made something for all important occasions in the lives of her friends and family. Everybody loved her cakes and one day she had the idea to share her recipes with other people around the world! She speaks English and so she thought, a lot of people worldwide could watch her videos that would show the making of international recipes, like a little "cake tour around the world".

If you want to find out, how it went with Josie's home baking video blog, start reading at number 1.

1 On Thursday Josie came home after spending the morning at summer camp and looked for her mother to tell her about her idea! She found her with her friend Cathrin in the garden doing yoga during lunch break. "Mum, Cathrin, I have to tell you something! I will have my own home baking video blog." "Wow, my dear, that's interesting news, I am happy for you. But you need to know there are risks and things you should be careful with. Don't tell people where you live", her mum said. "That's true", Cathrin agreed, "and in case you are successful with what you're doing, there will be haters posting negative comments."

2 Even though Josie lives in a small town, there is everything you need in your daily life. Apart from a supermarket, an organic shop, a coffee place, a stationery shop and a bike shop, there is also a flower shop where Josie's dad sometimes buys flowers. The florist who works there is really nice. For her blog, she wants to put beautiful flowers in the background of the photos. But that's something she can pay attention to when she has more followers and more routine. For this reason, Josie doesn't go to the flower shop today, please continue the tour somewhere else.

3 This was no easy decision ... Josie had always liked recipes from Asian countries. But she has never tried cakes from Asian countries ... mhhh ... She looked through her grandma's book and there it was – a recipe for a Japanese matcha cake. That would be her first video on the blog. Where could she get the best matcha? The decision for the second cake was easier: she wanted to prepare a carrot cake with cream cheese frosting and almonds on top. She wrote a shopping list and knew she would get most of the ingredients at the regular supermarket. She took her big rucksack and collected the products she needed for the two cakes. It took her a while because she was not as organised as her mum.

4 Back home, Josie started right away. She wanted to prepare the original carrot cake from her grandma. Of course, she knew it by heart because she had made it about a hundred times. You need: 400 grams of grated carrots, 250 grams of flour, 300 grams of sugar. She made the first cake in the kitchen without any major problems, the only difference was that it took her a lot longer than usually because she filmed every single step.

5 She nearly cried and didn't understand what she had done wrong. When she was sad or frustrated, she needed to talk to her mum who was upstairs in her office. Even though she was working she listened to Josie and tried to help her. "Josie, my dear, I know what the problem is. You know, grandma Sally's recipe book is quite old, and back then, the power of the oven was not like it is today. Each oven is different, so you have to know very well how strong yours is. With time you'll find out how long you really need to keep a cake in the oven in relation to grandma's recipes." So that was the problem! She had bought more ingredients than needed and could make a second cake. This time she found out that 20 minutes in her oven are enough for the matcha cake.

6 The vegan and gluten free baking needed a little more preparation. She did some research on the internet to find out how other people replaced non-vegan products because she had no idea what else to take for eggs. She read that many vegan bakeries replace them with "aquafaba" which is chickpeas water – interesting, she would try it! Her mum recommended to look for the vegan and gluten free products in the little organic food store in the city centre. Josie was lucky, the owner of the shop was helpful and so she got the needed products.

7 In this building you can find Josie's music school where her piano lessons take place. Her brother has guitar lessons here, but he is a lazy student and his guitar teacher is always a little angry when he finds out that he did not practise. Then Josie's mother is angry too because she says that the music lessons are expensive. The summer holidays have already started, so the music school is also closed and there are no lessons at the moment. Keep on searching the next location.

8 When she walked out of the supermarket, she realised that she didn't get two things: matcha and some special nuts. Where could she get them? She thought about it for a while … and had the life-saving idea! The little Japanese farmers shop she regularly passed by but had never entered before. She took her bike and rode just 15 minutes to the shop. Aaaand – she was lucky! She got both ingredients and was happy on her way back home to finally start baking.

9 A few days after the vegan and gluten free alternatives had gone on the video blog as well, Josie's mum asked her to go to her favourite coffee place to buy coffee beans for their coffee machine at home. When Josie entered the shop, the owner said: "I have seen your videos, they are great!" "Oh thank you", Josie answered. "Would you like to bake cakes for my café from time to time? I know you still go to school but like once a week or in the holidays? Everybody in the city is talking about your videos!", the owner added. Josie was happy! Of course, she said yes! Who would have imagined that her home baking video blog would be such a success? Josie had not!

10 This is the bike shop where Josie just had her bike repaired. She likes chatting with the owner, Tom, who had longer hair and looked like a surfer boy from Hawaii. In fact, he is from Denver, Colorado. Once a month, Tom offers people who do not have a lot of money to repair their bikes for free. So nice! Unfortunately, she doesn't have time to talk to Tom, she is on the way to find the ingredients for her cake, so please continue searching the way to the supermarket.

11 Josie went into the garage of her house because she didn't know that her mum was not keeping the vacuum cleaner here anymore. Their garage was huge with a lot more space than you need when you only have one car. Josie even thought about filming some of her videos here, but realised it was not a good idea so far away from the kitchen. Please go back to the kitchen, this is not the place where Josie will be filming her videos.

12 After she had finished the first video Josie was happy with the result. When the cake came out of the oven, she put the frosting on top and took pictures, then placed the cake on the dining room table and texted her family that everybody was allowed to take a piece. Then the more difficult part was about to start: the matcha cake. She mixed all the ingredients and put the mixture in the oven. The recipe said 30 minutes, Josie set the timer to 25 minutes. With the first time you better be safe.

13 You are at the bakery near Josie's house where she never buys cake or coffee for her parents. It's a chain company and the cake is not "homemade" but by a machine in a factory. Josie doesn't like cakes like that! She just sometimes comes here to buy a sandwich before school or when she's in a hurry going to her piano lessons right after school. Today she is not hungry and on her way to the supermarket to buy the products for her first videos, so please keep on searching the correct shop.

14 Josie was a bit sad after her mum's and Cathrin's warning but deep inside she knew they were right, and she had to be careful. She sat in the living room and called her dad at work to tell him about her plans and see what he thought about it. "Your mum and Cathrin are right, you have to be careful. But we think you are smart enough to be careful whenever it's necessary. We mentioned the risks and the rest is up to you. If you need help, let us know. "

15 In front of you there is Josie's school. She liked going there because she was a good student and liked to see her friends there. With the summer holidays she had the time to start her blog. Her plan was to make some videos before the holidays end so that she only needed to post them later. She also needed to find some people who ate all the cake because she was against wasting food. Her family could only eat a limited amount, so maybe she would ask the neighbours! But now go on searching the next place, at the moment Josie doesn't need to go to school.

16 On her way to the Japanese farmers shop she passed the new exclusive but super expensive French patisserie which had opened two months ago in her town. People said the cakes and croissants were very good but also incredibly expensive. Josie never tried them. Her mum kept on saying that she preferred Josie's cakes anyway. Today she did not enter, she was on the way to buy the products for her own cake, so please go on.

17 The next baking afternoon, now with the vegan and gluten free products, could not take place at home. Josie's mum had to prepare dinner for some friends who were coming over. Josie asked her grandma Sally, who lived next door, if she could use her kitchen. So Josie brought all the products to her kitchen and started baking. It was not easy because she was not used to make vegan or gluten free cakes. Especially the vegan one was not so easy. She had to replace the eggs, milk and cream cheese with vegan alternatives. It took her a while but then both cakes were in the oven and when they were ready and Josie tried them, she was happy with the result! Vegan baking? No problem for Josie!

18 This is the house of Sara's family, one of Josie's best friends. The two girls have known each other since kindergarten and have been very close friends since then. Last year Josie spent her summer holidays with Sara's family and they had a very nice time in Italy. This year, Sara's family went to Italy again but Josie's family had planned to go to France a little later and could not accompany Sara's family. For this reason, nobody is at home right now. Please go on searching.

19 You are in front of the town hall of Josie's hometown. If you need a new passport, a parking permit or have any other issue, you must go there. Usually, you need to wait quite a while because there are not enough people working there. Josie's brother sometimes worked there during the summer holidays to earn some money because he was a fast learner and easily managed to do his tasks. Today Josie is in a hurry. Go back to the last place.

20 After the two conversations with her parents, she was a little less enthusiastic about her project but nevertheless she decided to give it a try. Josie thought there were not many worse things than regretting decisions. The first step was to choose recipes for the first two videos. Filming a video was an effort and probably the kitchen would be pretty chaotic afterwards. Josie wanted to film two recipes at once for the first two blog entries. She sat on the floor in her room and looked at grandma Sally's old recipe book. She was so proud that grandma had given it to her a while ago.

21 This is another shop in town that Josie liked a lot, it belonged to her mother's friend Cathrin, a stationery shop. Josie often went there just to look at the things she sold and sometimes she even helped Cathrin with her work (when she didn't have too much to do for school). Right now, it's lunch time and the shop is closed. Cathrin is doing yoga with Josie's mother. So please go back to the last location.

22 When the cake was in the oven, she started preparing the icing made out of icing sugar, lemon, almonds and a little vanilla. Unfortunately, she realised that she didn't have enough icing sugar. Oh no, she didn't want to cycle to the supermarket once again! In the basement her mum keeps some products that do not expire so quickly like flour and pasta, so Josie went downstairs to see if she could also find some icing sugar. She was lucky, there was some on the last shelf. Back in the kitchen, the alarm clock rang and when she took the cake out of the oven, she could already see that the cake was burnt! But how could that happen? She had left it in the oven five minutes less?!

23 In the late afternoon, after having finished both cakes, she sat down with her family on the terrace to eat some cake. Her brother had just returned from a friend and her dad from work. She told them that she had uploaded her first two videos on the blog. "That's a cool project, Josie! I am quite excited to see how it will be going, little sister", her brother said. "Sounds like you had a good first day!", her dad added. Then Josie took her phone to check how many people had seen her videos. She was overwhelmed: 52,657 views in three hours – that was incredible! And so many nice comments. Some of them asked for a vegan or gluten free alternative to her recipes. "Well, that's my new challenge: creating a vegan and a gluten free version of my recipe!", she shouted.

My reading trail:

1												

Vocabulary

enthusiastic	begeistert, voller Vorfreude	**effort**	Herausforderung, Anstrengung
to expire	ablaufen	**occasion**	Gelegenheit
stationery shop	Schreibwarenladen	**pastry**	Gebäckstück
ingredients	Zutaten	**flour**	Mehl
to accompany	begleiten	**icing**	Glasur, Zuckerguss
parking permit	Parkausweis, Parkerlaubnis	**chickpeas**	Kichererbsen
nevertheless	nichtsdestotrotz	**to mention**	erwähnen

The home baking video blog
Lesespurgeschichte (2)

Carrot cake, brownies, New York cheesecake … Who doesn't like pastries, cake or cookies? Josie has always had a passion for baking and she recently developed a passion to bake something for important occasions in the lives of her friends and family. And guess what? Everybody loved her cakes! So one day she had the idea to share her recipes and her passion for baking with other people around the world! Since she speaks English, she thought, that a lot of people worldwide could watch her videos that would show the making of international recipes, like a little "cake tour around the world" on her blog.

If you want to find out, how it went with Josie's home baking video blog, start reading at number 1.

1 On Thursday Josie came home after spending the morning at summer camp and looked for her mother impatiently because she wanted to tell her the latest news about her idea! She found her in the garden doing yoga during her lunch break with her friend Cathrin. "Mum, Cathrin, I have to tell you something! I've thought about it for a while and now I decided to do it. I will have my own home baking video blog sharing recipes with people around the world." "Wow, my dear, that's interesting news. First, I am happy for you. But you need to know that there are risks also and things you need to be careful with. Don't tell people where you live, like the exact location of our house, you never know which burglar watches these videos", her mum claimed. "That's true", Cathrin agreed, "and one more thing is, in case you are successful with what you're doing, there will be haters posting mean comments. You should be aware of this before you start."

2 Even though Josie lives in a small town, there is everything you need in your daily life. Apart from a supermarket, an organic shop, a coffee place, a stationery shop and a bike shop, there is also a flower shop where Josie's dad sometimes buys flowers for her mother or her grandmother for special occasions like birthdays or Mother's Day. The florist who works there is really nice and Josie even thought about doing her next internship in his shop. For her blog, she thought about flower arrangements in the background of the photos or putting a vase with dry flowers in the background of her videos to make everything look nice. But step by step, that's something she can pay attention to when she has more followers and more routine. For this reason, Josie doesn't go to the flower shop today, please continue the tour somewhere else.

3 This was obviously not an easy decision … Josie had always liked recipes from Asian countries, she was a huge fan of curries or soups like pho or ramen. But when it came to cake she never tried one from Asian countries … mhhh … She looked through her grandma's book and there it was! Yes, that was it – a recipe for a Japanese matcha cake, that would be her first video on the blog. Cool! Where could she get the best matcha? The decision for the second cake was easier. Whenever somebody threw a party in her family or on occasion of her friends' birthday parties Josie was asked to prepare her legendary carrot cake with cream cheese frosting and roasted almonds on top. So she started a shopping list for the supermarket – the first steps were taken! She knew where to get most of the ingredients: right at the local supermarket where Josie's family also did their regular grocery shopping. She liked accompanying her mum or dad to the supermarket because she always managed to smuggle some of her favourite products (like mangoes, smoothies, yoghurts) in the shopping cart without her parents noticing. Today she went by herself, took her big hiking rucksack and collected the products she needed for the two cakes. It took her a while because she was not as organised as her mum (who always writes her shopping lists according to her way through the shop) and had to walk back and forth a few times.

4 Back home, Josie started right away. She needed to make profit from this motivation she felt. The process of baking is never the same: each time you prepare a cake, something is a little different. Sometimes you miss ingredients, you want to use up a product an take more of it or you want to try a new variation with a new frosting or taste but today Josie wanted to follow the original carrot cake recipe by her grandma without any experiments. She knew it by heart because she had made it nearly a hundred times. You need:

400 grams of grated carrots, 250 grams of flour, 300 grams of sugar. She made the first cake in the kitchen without any major problems, the only difference was that it took her a lot longer than usually because she filmed every single step, even repeating some steps because she didn't like the camera angle or the tone of her voice.

5 She was close to crying and didn't understand what she had done wrong. When she was sad or frustrated, she needed to talk to her mum who was upstairs in her office. Even though she was working she listened to Josie and tried to comfort her. "Josie, my dear, I know what the problem is. You know, grandma Sally's recipe book is quite old, so back then, the power of the oven was not like it is today. Each oven is different, so you have to know very well how strong yours is. With time you will find out how long you really need to keep a cake in the oven in relation to grandma's recipes." So that was the problem! Josie would have never thought about that! Luckily, she had bought more ingredients than she needed and made a second cake. This time she was very cautious, checking every two to three minutes if the cake was alright and so she found out that 20 minutes are enough in her oven for the matcha cake to be done.

6 The vegan and gluten free baking needed a little more preparation than Josie's first baking attempt. She researched on the internet how other people replaced non-vegan products because she had no idea what to use instead of, for example, eggs which were an essential ingredient in nearly every cake recipe Josie has. She read that many vegan bakeries replace eggs with "aquafaba" which is actually chickpeas water – that sounded interesting, she would try it! Her mum recommended to look for the vegan and gluten free products in the little organic food store in the city centre, so that's were Josie went. She was lucky, the owner of the shop was really helpful and she got all the products without any major problems. She promised the owner to mention the name of his shop in the video and left.

7 In this building you can find Josie's music school where her piano lessons take place. She has had lessons for five years now and she really loves it. Her brother has guitar lessons here, but he is a rather lazy student and his guitar teacher is always a little angry when he realises that he did not practise his latest songs. Then Josie's mother is angry too because she says that the music lessons are not cheap and she is not willing to pay for them any more if her son doesn't practise with more motivation. Since the summer holidays have already started, music school is also closed and lessons don't take place at the moment. Keep on searching the next location.

Where do the following cakes or pastries come from?

– Scones: ....

– Banana bread: ....

– Malasadas: ....

– Churros: ....

8 Walking out of the supermarket, she saw two things left on her list that she didn't get: matcha (very important for the MATCHA cake) and pecan nuts. Where could she get these products? She thought about it for a while and was close to postponing today's baking and order the products online. But they would probably arrive by the day after tomorrow and Josie was so motivated and badly wanted to start RIGHT AWAY! Then she had the life-saving idea! The little Japanese farmers shop where she regularly passed by but had never entered before. She took her bike and rode just 15 minutes to the shop. Aaaand – she was lucky! She got both ingredients and was happy on her way back home to finally start baking.

9 A few days after the vegan and gluten free alternatives had gone online as well, Josie's mum asked her to go to her favourite coffee place to buy coffee beans for their coffee machine at home. When Josie entered the shop, the owner, a very nice lady, came to her and seemed a little excited! "I have seen your videos, they are great, you are so creative", she said. "Oh thank you", Josie replied. "I have a question to ask – would you like to bake cakes for my café from time to time? I know you still go to school and you need to study but like once a week or in the holidays? I think my guests would be more than happy to try your cakes. Everybody in the city is talking about your videos!", the owner added. Josie was overwhelmed – what an offer! Of course, she said yes! Who would have imagined that her home baking video blog would be such a success? Josie had not!

10 This is the bike shop where Josie recently had her bike repaired because the brakes did not work properly – which is a high security risk. Josie really likes chatting with the cute owner of the bike shop, Tom, who had longer hair and looked like a surfer boy from Hawaii. In fact, he is from Denver, Colorado. Josie doesn't care, she likes the Hawaiian surfer boy idea. Once a month, Tom offers people who do not have a lot of money to repair their bikes for free. That's his personal social project and Josie thinks that this is really kind of him. But today, unfortunately, she doesn't have time to talk to Tom, she is on the way to find all the ingredients for her cake, so please continue searching the way to the supermarket.

11 Josie went into the garage of her house because she didn't know that her mum was not keeping the vacuum cleaner here anymore. Their garage was huge with a lot more space than you need when you only have one car like Josie's family. For a second she thought about setting up a little studio in one corner of the garage to make her videos because she liked the design of the bricks in the garage and thought that would be a nice background for the videos. But then she realised that without the stove and the oven in the kitchen it was impossible to prepare her cakes and she immediately dismissed the idea. So please go back to the kitchen, this is not the place where Josie will be filming her videos.

Can you guess? What is a "cronut"?

It's a mixture ....

12 After she had finished the first video Josie was happy and satisfied with the result. When the cake came out of the oven and had cooled a little, she put the frosting on top and took pictures from different angles. After that she put the cake on the dining room table and texted her family that everybody was allowed to take a piece. Then the more difficult part of today's task was about to start: the matcha cake. She mixed all the ingredients according to her grandma's recipe and put the mixture in the oven. The recipe said 30 minutes, Josie set the timer to 25 minutes. With the first time you better be safe.

13 You are at the bakery near Josie's house but here she never buys cake or coffee for her parents. The main reason is that this bakery is part of a chain so they have several bakeries in the area and the cake is not "homemade" or "self-made". The cakes and pastries are made by machines in a factory which Josie disapproves of. You can taste and feel they are not self-made and not made with love and passion. She comes here just sometimes to buy a sandwich before school or when she's in a hurry for her piano lessons right after school – and without lunch. Today she is not hungry and on her way to do grocery shopping for her first videos, so keep on searching the correct shop.

14 Josie was a bit sad after hearing her mum's and Cathrin's warning but deep inside she knew they were right, and she had to be careful. In school, they learnt about cyberbullying and hate speech and she knew that problem should not be underestimated when she was about to post things of her private life online. She sat in the living room and called her dad at work to tell him about her plans and see what he thought about it. To be honest, she knew the answer before she called him. "Your mum and Cathrin are right, you have to be careful. But of course, we will not forbid this because we think you are smart enough to be careful whenever it's necessary. We mentioned the risks and the rest is up to you. If you need help, let us know."

15 In front of you there is Josie's school that she really liked. She was a good and motivated student and liked seeing her friends there. With the summer holidays she had the time to start the project with her blog. Right now, she could not tell how much time she would have to run her blog when school started again but that was something she would worry about later. Her plan was to make some videos in advance so that she only needed to post them after a certain time. She only had to find some people who ate all the cake because she was against wasting food, and her family of four could only eat a limited amount of cake, of course. She might ask the neighbours in her street … but now go on searching the next place, at the moment Josie doesn't need to go to school.

16 On her way to the Japanese farmers shop she passed the new exclusive but super expensive French patisserie which had opened two months ago in her town. People said the tartes, macarons and croissants were incredibly good but also incredibly expensive, and Josie never had the chance to try them. Her mum always kept on saying that she preferred Josie's cakes anyway. The cakes they showed on display look incredibly good, that's what Josie can tell. But today, she did not enter, she was on the way to buy the products for her own cake, so please go on searching the ingredients.

17 The next baking afternoon, now with the vegan and gluten free products, could unfortunately not take place at home because Josie's mum had to prepare dinner for some friends that were coming over. For this reason, Josie had asked her grandma Sally, who lived next door, if she could use her kitchen. "Of course, you can, my dear", she said. So Josie brought all the products to her kitchen and started baking which was not easy because she was not very used to make vegan or gluten free cakes. The gluten free one was okay because she just used gluten free flour, the rest could stay the same. But the vegan one was difficult: she had to replace the eggs, milk and cream cheese with vegan alternatives and they usually have a different texture than non-vegan products. It took her a while but then the vegan cake was in the oven too and when both cakes were ready and Josie tried both of them, she was happy with the result! Vegan baking? No problem for Josie!

18 This is the house of Sara's family, one of Josie's best friends. The two girls have known each other since kindergarten and have been very close friends since then. Last year Josie was even allowed to spend her summer holidays with Sara's family and they had a very nice time in Italy. Every afternoon they enjoyed good Italian cakes, Sara's parents had coffee and the girls fresh orange lemonade. La dolce vita! This year, Sara's family went to Italy again but Josie's family had planned to go to France a little later and so she didn't have time to accompany Sara's family again. For this reason, nobody is at home right now. Please go on searching.

19 You are in front of the town hall of Josie's hometown. If you need a new passport, a parking permit for residents or have any other issue, you must go there. Usually, you need to wait quite a while because there are not enough people working there. Josie's brother sometimes worked there during the summer holidays to earn some money because he was a fast learner and easily managed to do his tasks. Josie once went to the town hall to ask the mayor if the town had money to modernise the playground next to her school but today, she is in a hurry finding the ingredients for her cakes. Go back to the last place.

Find the best name for Josie's home baking video blog! Take a vote in class afterwards!

20 After the two conversations with her parents, she was a little less enthusiastic about her project but nevertheless she decided to give it a try. She knew, otherwise she would keep on thinking about it saying to herself "what would have happened if I had only tried it …". Josie thought there were not many worse things than regretting decisions. So, the decision was taken! The first step was to choose recipes for the first two videos. Filming a video was an effort and probably the kitchen would be pretty chaotic afterwards which was why Josie wanted to film two recipes at once for the first two blog entries. She sat on the floor in her room and looked at grandma Sally's old recipe book which she kept like a little treasure. She was so proud that grandma had given it to her a while ago.

21 This is another shop in town that Josie liked a lot, it belonged to her mother's friend Cathrin, a stationery shop. Josie often went there to just look at the things she sold and sometimes she even helped Cathrin with her work (when she didn't have too much to do for school). She liked to help the customers with finding rulers, pencils or cards because she knew where everything was in the shop. Cathrin had even had the idea to offer a creative workshop for primary school children and she had already asked Josie if she wanted to help her. Right now, it's lunch time so Cathrin keeps the shop close. She is doing yoga with Josie's mother to reduce her stress level. So please go back to the last location.

22 When the cake was in the oven, she started preparing the icing made out of icing sugar, lemon, almonds and a little vanilla. Unfortunately, she realised that she didn't have enough icing sugar. Oh no, she was really not in the mood to cycle to the supermarket once more and stand in the queue again. In the basement her mum keeps some products that do not expire so quickly like flour, pasta or canned tomatoes, so Josie went downstairs to see if she could also find some icing sugar. She was lucky, she found some on the last shelf. It had already expired but she didn't care, it's only icing sugar and nothing fresh. She knew from her mum that most products do not really expire at the date the packaging tells you. Back in the kitchen, the alarm clock rang and when she took the cake out of the oven, she could already see the mess! The cake was burnt! But how could that happen? She had left the cake in the oven five minutes less?!

In the US, the recipes use different units. They do not say "grams" or "kilograms" but cups.

If you want to weigh flour, have a look at the following chart and fill in the missing parts:

grams	cups
	1/8
	1/4
	1/2
120	

23 In the late afternoon, after having finished both cakes, she sat down with her family on the terrace to eat some cake. Her brother had just returned from a friend and her dad from work. She told them about the process and that she had uploaded her first two videos on the blog. In order to get more followers, she had posted a link to the blog in her social media profile that could also be reposted by her friends and other people she knew. "That's a cool project, Josie! I am quite excited to see how it will be going, little sister", her brother said. "Sounds like you had a good first day! I just hope you have our warnings in mind", her dad added. Then Josie took her phone to check how many people had seen her videos and if somebody had left a comment. She was overwhelmed: 52,657 views in three hours – that was incredible! And so many nice comments. Some of them were interesting because they asked for a vegan or gluten free alternative to her recipes. "Well, that's my new challenge: creating a vegan and a gluten free version of my recipe", she said enthusiastically.

My reading trail:	1												

The home baking video blog
Lösungen

My reading trail:	1	14	20	3	8	4	12	22	5	23	6	17	9

Solutions:

Riddle to **7**: Scones: England, Banana bread: Australia/USA, Malasadas: Portugal (eaten a lot in Hawaii as well), Churros: Spain (and Latin America)

Riddle to **11**: A "cronut" is a mixture between a **croissant** and a **doughnut**.

Riddle to **19:** individual answers

Riddle to **22:**

grams	cups
15	1/8
30	1/4
60	1/2
120	1

Sherlock Holmes in London
Lesespurlandkarte

Sherlock Holmes in London
Lesespurgeschichte (1)

This story is about the famous detective Sherlock Holmes. As everybody knows, he solves his cases with the help of his partner and good friend Dr Watson. They got to know each other a long time ago, found out they are good partners and started working together. Today, a mysterious-looking man entered Holmes' office and asked for help.

If you want to know, what the man told him and which case they had to solve, start reading at number 1.

1 "Mr Holmes, I really need your help", said the m**a**$_{10}$n. "What happened?", Holmes asked. "My daughter Gloria disappeared, I think she is somewhere in East London, you know, there was this man who seemed to be nice but he might have forced her to go there", Mr Johnson, that was the man's name, answered. "Wait", Holmes stopped him, "please start from the beginning, otherwise I cannot follow." So Mr Johnson told him about the man his daughter had met at a soirée in one of the duke's houses where she was working as a waitress that evening. She was impressed because the man was good-looking and she agreed to meet him the following day. Now Mr Johnson did not know where his daughter was.

2 Cricket is also a very popular sport in London. That's why there are some cricket grounds where people can play. Right now you are at the biggest cricket ground in London. Holmes and Watson were both interested in horse races but not in cricket and so they didn't even think about looking for Gloria here. Please continue somewhere else.

3 When Mr Johnson left, Holmes went into the hallway of his small flat and call**e**$_{2}$d Watson. "Watson, man, we've got a case, you must come over. We need to find the daughter of a man called Mr Johnson in the east of the city. Please hurry up, we don't know if the girl is in danger", he told Watson on the phone. "Oh hello Holmes, my friend, I was about to read my newspaper, but I will come to help you, let me just finish my morning tea", Watson answered.

4 Close to the pub was the famous Old Spitalfields Market where you could buy nearly everything. Since it was not far away from the Royal Oak, they went in this direction and walked around the market stalls. They asked an older woman selling eggs if she knew something about the man. They ha**d**$_{4}$ no luck. Another chat with a man selling vegetables ended with the same result: only disappointment! At least the man from the vegetable stall suggested to talk to the owner of a little book shop in Redchurch Street because he knew a lot of people in town.

5 In front of you is the big post office of Centra**l**$_{9}$ London. From here, people can send postcards or letters to people worldwide. Sometimes they arrive, but sometimes they don't. Holmes always sent letters to his brother Mycroft Holmes from this post office when he was not in town. Right now, Mycroft was in London, so Holmes didn't need to send him any letters. Go back to the last position and continue the search somewhere else.

6 It was already dark and they couldn't see anything, so they went towards a lantern because they wanted to look at the map. The lantern stood in front of the street signs where Emerald and Southend Road met. A man with a hood appeared from behind and Holmes and Watson were afraid. "Sorry, but I heard you are searching General Williams and this girl. I think I can help you", the man said. "This morning, I w**a**$_{3}$s walking around the old butchery two streets further east. It is a very quiet place since the butchery was closed some months ago. But most of the doors to old factory rooms are not locked and you can just ente**r**$_{1}$. I hid when I heard voices coming closer, but I saw a young lady with blonde hair. This could be the girl and the man you are searching." "Thank you so much for your help. We owe you something!", Watson said and they hurried to the butchery.

7 London has many great museums and Holmes and Watson liked spendin**g**$_{8}$ time there. Holmes' favourite museum was the Natural History Museum, whereas Watson preferred the National Gallery because he loved paintings. Right now, you are in front of the National History Museum in South Kensington but the two detectives didn't have time for a visit, they had to find Gloria. Besides, a museum is no place for hiding: there are many guard**s**$_{12}$ to watch over the paintings. Please go back to the last place.

8 Here you can see Hyde Park, the biggest park in Central London. It is huge and during the night there are strange people hanging around. But our two detectives were focused on the east part of the city to find Gloria. Go back to the east of the city to continue the search!

9 Out of breath they arrived at the front gate of the old butchery. It was a very dark and mystic place. They quietly walked around old containers and equipment, already full of rust. From one of the cellars, they could hear voices and they went to its door. Holmes counted from one to three with his fingers and then they opened the door with a rush. There was only one man who was so shocked to see somebody that he dropped his pistol and nearly had a heart attack. Watson tied up his hands while Holmes freed Gloria who was tied to a chair with a rope. "Are you Gloria? We are so glad to see you healthy without injuries!", Holmes said.

10 Watson arrived and the two men went straight to Holmes' small library for a map of London. They unfolded the map on the small table in the corner of the little room. Watson pushed over the candle so that it nearly hit the map and Holmes had to shout at him: "Be careful, man! You will set my library on fire." They looked at the map and discussed where to start. They agreed the best spot was the area around Shoreditch High Street: there are many restaurants or pubs with lots of people around.

11 In front of you, there is the police station of the city of London. Of course, many people would call the police if they were in Mr Johnson's situation. In our case, th**i**$_{5}$s is no likely option. Mr Johnson asked Holmes and Watson for help: he obviously didn't want to talk to the police. Moreover, Holmes and Watson were self-confident and experienced enough to find Gloria without the help of the police. Go on, this is not the correct place.

12 When they found Gloria, the girl was still shaking but was so relieved when she heard Holmes and Watson had been sent by her father. "Oh, thank you so much, this man was keeping me here against my will and wanted to bring me to France as his second wife. Thank you again!", Gloria cried. They brought her back to her father's house. He had tears in his eyes when he put his arms around his daughter. He also thanked Holmes and Watson a hundred times!

13 In the city centre, around Trafalgar Square it was too crowded to find somebody or to talk to people. In the middle of Trafalgar Square there is a huge statue of Admiral Nelson. Unfortunately, this is not the place where Holmes and Watson continued their search, it was too confusing and too busy. Besides, if something happened in this part of the city, there would be so many people around that a criminal could write about his plans in the newspaper. So please head back to the east where Watson and Holmes continued their search.

14 Holmes and Watson asked themselves why they had not had this idea on their own. The red light district was a smart idea! Again, this was a dark area of the town with a lot of dangerous, mysterious people in the streets or in the little pubs. Especially Watson did not like this gloomy area, he didn't feel safe. They stood at the beginning of the street known as the red light district and looked around. They consulted their map again to plan their search.

15 Now you arrived at Buckingham Palace, the home of the British Royals. This is no place to hide a kidnapped person because around Buckingham Palace there are always guards with weapons. Watson and Holmes had to hurry up to find Gloria, so please continue back on track.

16 This is a pub in the east of London. Usually they would have entered to talk to people and check if somebody knew more about Gloria or the man. Unfortunately, Holmes must not enter this pub due to one of his older cases. He found out something about the owner of the pub who was in prison afterwards and hat do serve time. Now Holmes must not get inside anymore, so please continue the search somewhere else.

17 What a view of the Thame**s**$_{11}$ river! This was Holmes' favourite place, a bench right at the bank of the river with a beautiful view of the city. He often came here to think about a problem or to get fresh air. But Holmes and Watson were in a hurry and could not come here for a break. They knew Gloria would not sit on a bench in the middle of the city. Please go back to the last place.

18 The search was on! Holmes and Watson left Holmes' flat and started the tour. On their way to the east they passed the famous Globe Theatre. They spontaneously decided to have a look inside, for it had dark and shady alleys and rooms behind the stage where you could easily hide someone. They wandered around the whole area of the theatre but after some minutes they realised that Gloria was not hidden there. Good first try – go on!

19 You arrived at St Paul's Cathedral in London. From the top of the church visitors have a great view! Watson was not a very religious person and didn't go to church often. Moreover, a church was not the best place to hide someone because there were many people around. Even though St Paul's Cathedral was an interesting place, the two detectives did not continue their search here, so go back to the last location and keep on looking for Gloria!

20 Holmes and Watson walked to the small book shop in Redchurch Street. The book shop was impressive and had a mystic atmosphere. "Sir, I am Sherlock Holmes, this is my friend and assistant Dr Watson. We are looking for a girl called Gloria and a man with brown hair and a height of 1,75 m. Have you heard anything about them or maybe even seen them?", Holmes asked the owner. But the man had not heard anything about them. Instead he had an idea: the red light district!

21 "The Royal Oak" – what a name for a pub! After the first stop at the Globe Theatre, the Royal Oak was the seco**n**$_{6}$d stop of the two detectives. "Watson, you talk to all the people in the back of the pub and I stay in the front close to the bar, okay?", Holmes suggested. Holmes' first step always was talking to the owner of the pub behind the bar. He sees a lot of people every day and after some beers many people get talkative and tell him about private things. Unfortunately, today they did not get any useful information!

22 London has more than one train station. Here you are at King's Cross where many trains arrive, so it is a very busy place. In a train station there are lots of corners, little rooms or other places to hide someone, but there are so many people around. Usually, there are also several police officers to check if everyone is alright. All this considered, they won't find Gloria in this train station.

23 In front of you is London's famous horse racing arena! Every Saturday or Sunday the important people in town met here to watch the horse races and bet which horse would win. Holmes and Watson have already been to such races and liked it. Today, there were riders practising on their horses, their trainers and also people from the local newspapers, so it was very busy and crowded. Besides, there was no space to hide someone. You are at the wrong location here, go on searching somewhere else.

24 After he got to know the first details, Holmes invited the man in to his livin**g**$_{7}$ room and sit down next to the fireplace. "Now I understand the problem, but why do you think we can find her in East London?", Holmes asked. "Because I heard that this man lives in the east of the town and regularly visits people there." "Okay, that's a good first hint, I will ask my assistant and friend Dr Watson to come and join me." "Yes, please, go ahead and hurry up! I am so worried about my daughter!"

My reading trail:

1											

Solution word: Sometimes, when Sherlock Holmes could not find his glasses, he had to use a .... to read a book with small letters.

Vocabulary

soirée	festliche Abend-veranstaltung	**to bet**	wetten
butchery	Metzgerei	**gloomy**	düster, dunkel
waitress	Kellnerin	**cellar**	Keller
lantern	Laterne	**alley**	Gang, Korridor
hood	Kapuze	**talkative**	gesprächig
red light district	Rotlichtviertel	**bench**	Bank
relieved	erleichtert	**likely**	wahrscheinlich

Sherlock Holmes in London
Lesespurgeschichte (2)

This story is about the world-famous detective Holmes, Sherlock Holmes to be more precise. As everybody knows, he solves his cases with the help of his partner and good friend Dr Watson. They got to know each other a long time ago, found out they are good partners and started collaborating since then. Today, a mysterious-looking man entered Holmes' office and asked for help.

If you want to know, what the man tells him and which case they had to solve, start reading at number 1.

1 "Mr Holmes, I urgently need your help", said the m**a**$_{10}$n in a desperate and excited voice. "What happened, Sir?", Holmes asked. "My daughter Gloria went missing, she disappeared, I think she is somewhere in East London, you know, there was this man who seemed so charming at first glance and I think he forced her to go there …", the man, whose name was Mr Johnson, said without pausing. "Wait", Holmes stopped him, "please start from the beginning, otherwise I cannot follow." So Mr Johnson told him about the man his daughter had met at a soirée in one of the duke's houses where she was working as a waitress that evening. She was obviously impressed by his smartness, charming manners and character and immediately agreed to meet him the following day. Now Mr Johnson did not know where his daughter was.

2 Not only horse riding is a popular sport in London, but cricket too. Londoners play cricket since the 16th century and therefore there are some cricket grounds where people can enjoy their favourite game. Right now you are at the biggest cricket ground in London where the national cricket tournament takes place annually. Holmes and Watson were both interested in horse races but cricket was not really their cup of tea and so they didn't even think about having a look at this place to find Gloria. Please continue somewhere else.

3 When Mr Johnson left, Holmes went into the hallway of his small apartm**e**$_{2}$nt and called Watson. "Watson, man, we've got a case! Hurry up and come over. We need to find the daughter of a man called Mr Johnson, the search will lead us to the east of the city first. You better hurry up, we don't know if the girl is in danger", he told Watson on the phone. "Oh hello Holmes, my dearest friend, I was just about to read my beloved newspaper, but I will rush to help you. Let me just finish the last sip of my morning tea", Watson replied.

4 Close to the pub was the famous Old Spitalfields Market where you could buy pretty much everything from fresh fruits and vegetables to hot meals, clothes, books or jewellery. Since it was not far away from the Royal Oak, they went in this direction and strolled around the market stalls. They talked to an older woman selling eggs, to see if she knew something about the man who probably escaped with Gloria. They ha**d**$_{4}$ no luck. Another chat with a man selling vegetables ended with the same result: only disappointment, he hadn't seen or heard about Gloria and the man. At least the man from the vegetable stall had the idea to talk to the owner of a little book shop in Redchurch Street who knew a lot of people in town.

5 In front of you is the big post office of Centra**l**$_{9}$ London. From here, people can send postcards or letters to people worldwide. Sometimes they arrive, but sometimes they don't. Letters in Europe are delivered a lot quicker than letters to other continents. Holmes always sent letters to his brother Mycroft Holmes from this post office when he was not in town and he wanted to tell him something about one of his cases. Right now, Mycroft was in London, so Holmes didn't need to send him a letter. Writing a letter also takes a lot of time and Holmes was busy searching Gloria. Go back to the last position and continue the search somewhere else.

6 It was already dark and they couldn't see anything, so they stepped a few metres towards a lantern because they wanted to look at the map. The lantern stood in front of the street signs where Emerald and Southend Road met. While they were standing there, a man with a hood on his head crept up from behind so that Holmes and Watson got a fright. "Sorry, to bother you, but I heard you are searching General Williams and this girl. I think I can help you", the man said with a hoarse voice. "This morning, I w**a**$_{3}$s at the old butchery two streets further east. It is a very quiet place since the butchery was closed some months ago. But most of the doors to old factory rooms are not locked and you can just ente**r**$_{1}$. I hid when I heard voices coming closer, but I caught a glimpse of a young lady with blonde hair. It might have been the girl and the man you are searching." "Thank you so much for your help, we owe you something!", Watson said and they hurried to the butchery.

7 London has many great museums and Holmes and Watson also liked spendin**g**$_{8}$ time there. Holmes favourite museum was the Natural History Museum since he was interested in history, whereas Watson rather preferred the National Gallery because he loved paintings. Right now, you are in front of the National History Museum in South Kensington. The detectives didn't have time to enter and look at the current exhibition because they had to find Gloria. Besides, a museum is not a good place to hide someone: there are many guard**s**$_{12}$ who keep an eye on the visitors, so they don't damage or steal the exhibits. Please go back to the last place.

8 Here you can see Hyde Park, the biggest park in Central London. At first glance it seems likely to find somebody here because it is so huge and during the night there are gloomy people hanging around. But today our two detectives were rather focused on the east part of the city when when they tried to find Gloria. Who knows, without any success, they might have come back. Now go back to the east of the city to continue the search!

At the end of the 19th century, when Sherlock Holmes experienced his adventures, the English language was different because languages are constantly changing. Old English is the earliest recorded form of the English language, spoken in England in the early Middle Ages.

Can you guess the meaning of the following old English words in modern English?

sped: ....

woruld: ....

betweox: ....

fæmne: ....

halig: ....

hund: ....

9 Out of breath, they arrived at the front gate of the old butchery. With only a few rays of light of an old lantern it was a very gloomy and mystic place. Watson had to admit he was glad not to be alone around here in the evening. They quietly walked around the area of the old butchery past old containers and equipment which was already full of rust. From one of the cellars, they could hear voices and they silently approached its door. Without a sound Holmes counted from one to three and then they opened the door with a rush. There was only one man who was so shocked to see somebody that he dropped his pistol and nearly had a heart attack. Watson tied up his hands while Holmes freed Gloria who was tied to a chair with a rope. "Are you Gloria? We are so glad to see you healthy without injuries!", Holmes said.

10 Watson arrived and the two men went to Holmes' small library for a map of London. They unfolded the map on the small table in the corner of the little room. Watson pushed over the candle so that it nearly hit the map and Holmes had to shout at him: "Be careful, man! You will set my library on fire." They looked at the map and different places to clarify if it was worth a try and search the young lady Gloria there or not. Then they stuck little pins to the places they wanted to check and discussed the best route. They agreed to start searching the area around Shoreditch High Street, there are many restaurants or pubs with lots of people hanging around and passing by.

11 In front of you is the police station of the city of London. Of course, calling the police in a situation like this is the first option for people in need. In our case, th**i**$_{5}$s is not very likely. Mr Johnson asked Holmes and Watson for help, he obviously didn't want to talk to the police or didn't trust them to find his daughter. Moreover, Holmes and Watson were self-confident and experienced enough to find Gloria without the help of the police. Go on, this is not the correct place.

12 When they found Gloria, the girl was still shaking but relieved to hear Holmes and Watson had been sent by her father. "Oh, thank you so much, this man was keeping me here against my will and planned to bring me to France as his second wife. I cannot believe this nightmare is over. Thank you again!", Gloria cried. They brought her back to her father's house who was already impatiently waiting for the detectives and his girl. He had tears in his eyes when he finally put his arms around his beloved daughter and learned that she was not injured or harmed in any way. He also thanked Holmes and Watson a hundred times and promised he would come over the following day to talk about the salary.

13 In the city centre, around Trafalgar Square it was too crowded to find somebody or to talk to people. In the middle of Trafalgar Square there is a huge statue of Admiral Nelson which commemorates his victory at the Battle of Trafalgar in 1805. Unfortunately, this is not the place where Holmes and Watson continued their search, it was too confusing and too busy. People were rushing in all directions and there was hardly a calm corner. Besides, if something happened in this part of the city, there would be so many witnesses that a criminal could directly write about his plans in the local newspaper. So please head back to the east where Watson and Holmes continued their search.

According to the stories, Sherlock Holmes is a very clever and smart person who has a lot of different skills. Watson states that his favourite detective has knowledge of

as ...., **bo** ...., **ch** ....,

li .... **and po** ....**.**

14 Holmes and Watson wondered why they had not had this idea on their own. Of course, the red light district! That was a smart idea. Full of motivation, they quickened their pace and walked in the direction of the red light district. Again, this was a rather shady, dark area of the town with a lot of dangerous, mysterious people in the streets or in the little taverns. Especially Watson did not like this area at all, he didn't feel safe and there were women stepping up to him and offering him their service. They stood at the beginning of the street known as the red light district and looked around not knowing where to start their search. They wanted to have another look at their map to set up a more organised plan.

15 Now you arrived at Buckingham Palace, the home of the British Royals. If the British flag was hoisted on top of the palace people knew that Queen Victoria was at home. This is not the place to easily hide someone that was kidnapped because Buckingham Palace is probably the most guarded place in town: there are always guards with weapons around the whole building. An interesting thing to look at was the moment when the guards were changing, the so called "changing of the guards". Today, Holmes and Watson didn't have time for interesting activities like this, but had to hurry up to find Gloria, so please continue back on track.

16 This is a pub in the east of London, usually they would have entered to talk to people and check if somebody knew more about Gloria or her admirer. Unfortunately, Holmes was not allowed to enter this pub anymore because of one of his older cases. When he was in the pub due to his investigations, he found out something about the owner of the pub who ended up in prison. Now he was free again, but Holmes was not allowed in anymore, so please continue the search somewhere else.

17 What a view of the Thames river! This was Holmes' favourite place, a bench right at the bank of the river with a beautiful view of the city. He often came here when he was stuck with his inve**s**$_{11}$tigations and quietly wanted to think about a problem or just escape the darkness of his small flat. Today, Holmes and Watson were in a hurry, so they didn't have time to come here for a break. They knew that Gloria would not be sitting on a bench in the middle of the city. Please go back to the last place.

If Sherlock Holmes was a detective in 2024, what would be different? Come up with some ideas!

→ ……………………………………

→ ……………………………………

→ ……………………………………

→ ……………………………………

18 The search is on! Holmes and Watson left Holmes' flat and started the tour. Of course, it started raining and they had to take out their umbrellas to stay dry. On their way to the east they passed the famous Globe Theatre where Shakespeare plays were performed. This was no point on their map list, but they spontaneously decided to have a look inside the theatre, as it had long, dark alleys and small, shady rooms behind the stage where you could easily hide someone that must not be found. They wandered around the whole area of the theatre but after a few minutes they must acknowledge that Gloria was obviously not hidden in the Globe Theatre. Good first try – go on!

19 You arrived at St Paul's Cathedral in London with its huge dome. From the top of the church visitors have a great view! Watson was not a very religious person and didn't go to church that often. Moreover, a church was not the best place to hide someone because there were so many people around: people attending the service, tourists who took an interest in the architecture of the church, the priest, other people who work there … Even though St Paul's Cathedral was a very interesting place in town, the two detectives did not continue their search here, so go back to the last location and keep on looking for Gloria!

20 Holmes and Watson started their way to the small book shop in Redchurch Street since they did not have any other idea. The book shop was impressive, tall shelves up to the ceiling full of old and colourful books, some with golden bindings. On top of every shelf there was a little wooden sign indicating the topic of the literature: medicine, travel, French, drama, religion … It was a mystic atmosphere in here. "Sir, I am Sherlock Holmes and this is my friend and assistant Dr Watson. We are looking for a girl called Gloria and a man with brown hair, a height of 1,75m and a powerful stature. Have you heard anything about them or maybe seen them?", Holmes asked the owner of the bookshop. They were not lucky, the man had not heard anything either, like the other people they talked to before. But he had an idea: the red light district. When in doubt and in search of dubious people, the red light district is the place to go.

21 "The Royal Oak" – what a name for a pub! Pubs were a good place for investigations with lots of people watching other people or observing what went on outside. So, the Royal Oak was the second stop. "Watson, you talk to all the people in the back of the pub and I stay in the front close to the bar, okay?", Holmes suggested and the two men went separate ways inside. Holmes' first step always was talking to the pub owner behind the bar si**n**$_{6}$ce he sees a lot of people every day and after a pint or two everybody usually gets talkative. Today they did not get any useful information, even though the pub owner thought he might know the man in question but hasn't seen him in a while.

22 London, like most big cities, has more than one train station. Here you are at King's Cross where many long-distance trains arrive or depart, it is a very busy place. In a train station there are lots of corners, little rooms or other places where you could hide someone, but there are so many people around who will most likely disturb you. There are also several police officers walking around checking if everyone is alright because pickpockets have become a major problem at this place. For these reasons, one can be sure that Gloria has not been hidden somewhere in this train station.

23 In front of you is London's famous horse racing arena! Every Saturday or Sunday the noble people in town met here to watch the horse races and bet which horse would win. Holmes and Watson had been invited to attend such an event in the past because they knew some very famous people in London due to their job. They liked watching the horse race as it was pretty exciting and Watson even won some money with a bet. Today, there were professional riders and jockeys practising on their horses, the trainers and also people from the local newspapers, so it was busy and crowded. Besides, there was no space to hide someone. So you are wrong here, go somewhere else.

24 After this first introduction of the problem, Holmes invited the man in to his livin**g**$_7$ room and sit down next to the fireplace. "Now I understand the problem, but why do you think we can find her in East London?", Holmes asked. "That's because I asked everybody I know if they knew something about this man. I heard that he lives in the east of the town and regularly visits people there." "Okay, that's a good first hint, I will ask my assistant and friend Dr Watson to join me when we start searching your daughter. So you agree that we see it as our case to find your daughter and start our search?" "Yes, please, go ahead and hurry up! I am so worried about my daughter!"

My reading trail:

1											

Solution word: Sometimes, when Sherlock Holmes could not find his glasses, he had to use a .... to read a book with small letters.

Sherlock Holmes in London
Lösungen

My reading trail:	1	24	3	10	18	21	4	20	14	6	9	12

Solution word: **reading glass**

Solutions:

Riddle to **8**: sped: quickness, woruld: world, betweox: between, fæmne: woman, halig: holy, hund: dog

Riddle to **13**: According to the stories, Sherlock Holmes is a very clever and smart person who has a lot of different skills. Watson states that his favourite detective has knowledge of **astronomy**, **botany**, **chemistry**, **literature** and **politics**.

Riddle to **17**: individual answers

Geocaching in Central Park
Lesespurlandkarte

Geocaching in Central Park
Lesespurgeschichte (1)

Last Friday, the six friends Amir, Peter, Sophie, Lauren, Hailey and Josh finally found time for an activity they had in mind for a long time: geocaching in Central Park! Before they left, they discussed the groups. It turned out that Amir, Sophie and Josh would be one team as well as Peter, Lauren and Hailey.

If you want to find out, who won the geocaching adventure and if the friends liked it, start reading at number 1.

1 In the subway Sophie was excited and told Lauren: "I am a bit sad that we won't be in the same group. I would have loved to do this activity with you!" "Yes, me too. But now I am curious which team wins!", Lauren answered. Our six friends could see young boys with skateboards, families with picknick baskets, people with frisbees and skates. It was a beautiful day for outdoor activities in Manhattan! Of course, there were many tourists in the subway – but that's New York.

2 Here is another famous place in Central Park and something we can find all over Manhattan: a hot dog food stall! It's a cheap snack that many people buy after a day of sightseeing in the city. That's why the hot dog food stall in Central Park is always crowded. Our friends also liked to quickly grab a hot dog when they were hungry. Today they didn't do so because they had to continue their search and the tablet didn't lead them to this place. Go back to the last location and continue the way in another direction.

3 "Sorry boys, but it was so urgent", Sophie said while leading the group to the next place. Behind some trees she saw where their way would go: to the Alice in Wonderland Statue! That was also one of Sophie's favourite places in Central Park because she loved the story of Alice in Wonderland. Around the statue there were always groups of people enjoying coffee, cold drinks or ice cream. When the three friends arrived, the map showed them the coordinates for the last place!

4 The employee of the geocaching company was a nice guy of 25. The friends explained that they had already split up in two groups and they would do a competition and see who arrived faster! "Good idea, guys, this way geocaching is a lot more fun! Of course, the winning group who finds the geocache will get OUR reward", Tom, the boss of GeocachNY, laughed. Then he gave them two tablets, one to Amir and one to Hailey. Then Tom asked them inside to watch a short introduction video.

5 "Espressooooo, Latteeee, Cappuccinooo …", a man shouted. That was the famous coffee bike of an old Italian guy who loved to share his passion for good coffee. He often parked his coffee bike next to one of the playgrounds. Even though he was a funny person, our friends didn't drink coffee yet and with the help of the map on their tablet they found out that this was not the correct place. So please go on searching.

6 Once they got closer to Central Park Zoo, Josh started looking for the exact coordinates of their next POI where the following hint would be revealed. This was not easy at all! Josh got extremely ambitious after the first minutes of the geocaching race and after Sophie had explained in detail how to read the coordinates correctly. Their search led the three friends to the Safari Playground afterwards. That beautiful playground was surrounded by trees and it got its name because of the grey hippo statues children can climb on.

7 In front of you, you can see the Great Lawn, which was always full of people playing frisbee, lying on blankets or doing a picknick. It was a very nice place for a break after a long day at work or school. Sophie knew straight away that this was no good spot for a geocaching location because of the crowds that gathered here. You have to continue the search somewhere else, this is not the correct place.

8 On that little pond in the park is Gapstow Bridge. From there you have a nice view of the skyline of Manhattan. Today Sophie and her group did not pass the bridge and this pond since their coordinates did not tell them to. They must hurry to find the cache because they wanted to finish first. Continue finding the correct way and go back to the last location.

9 "I am sure there is only one more place that we need to go to, my feeling says so", Sophie said. "But friends, I am sorry, before we continue I really need to go to the toilet. Does anybody know where the public restrooms are in this park?" "Jesus, Sophie, can't you hold on until we finish the geocaching?", Amir asked. "No, I CANNOT", Sophie shouted and followed the signs for the restrooms. It took them five minutes until they arrived and then she also had to wait in line. When she came out, she took the tablet from Josh and followed the new directions.

10 Amir and Josh immediately climbed on two of the hippos! Sophie just shook her head and focused on the map to find the next piece of information for their search. The Safari Playground was never crowded, probably therefore it was part of the activity. "We need to go north … it looks like we would be somewhere around the Delacorte Theatre", Sophie said. She was right, after a short walk they reached the theatre where a performance for kids was on. What a nice atmosphere! They continued their way behind the stage when the map revealed the next point of interest.

11 When Sophie, Amir and Josh came back to the picknick area next to the house of the geocaching company, the others were already waiting there. "Oh no, I told you, they were faster. Sophie, that's only because you had to go to the toilet!", Amir complained. Again, Sophie had to calm herself down, to not shout at Amir, the idiot! "Amir, stop being such a bad loser and shouting at poor Sophie, we were just the better team. Accept it!", Lauren answered. The second team told the others that in the cache there was actually nothing special. But that's normal for geocaching, it's not about the prize but the journey is the reward!

12 You arrived at the Tennis Center in Central Park which is a nice place to play tennis. Josh liked playing tennis but today they didn't have time for activities like this! Their map told them to go in another direction and change their way. Here they were not at the correct location even though it was also interesting to look through the fence and watch the people play tennis. Some of them were really good!

13 On their way to the address of the company Amir suddenly started to sing "It's a beautiful day … hey hey … It's a beautiful day …" And the others sang along! "Oh no, look at the clouds up there, I hope it won't rain", Sophie said with a worried expression. "Oh Sophie, pleeeease, don't be so pessimistic", Amir said. "Don't worry, Soph, I am sure it won't rain and if so, I have an umbrella that you can take or we'll ask the company if they have rain capes." When they passed a small kiosk, Sophie decided to buy a small umbrella!

14 Up at the subway station when the friends got out of the train, they quickly needed to check their phones to see where they could find the little house of the geocaching company. They give you all the equipment, a short introduction about security and explain what you have to do if there is a problem. There are always employees of the company around the park who can quickly be there with their electric scooters and help you if you cannot continue. Josh found it and led the group in the correct direction.

15 Sophie tried to stay calm after Amir's mean comment. Amir and Josh were already busy trying to read the coordinates correctly and "translate" what the digital map said about the reality they saw. "Let me have a look", Sophie said, took the tablet, turned it around a few times until she knew in which direction to go. After a few minutes walk they had to change the direction again, then they arrived at the first POI (point of interest): the strawberry fields, a memorial for John Lennon, the lead singer of the Beatles.

16 You are in front of the statue of the famous Danish fairytale writer Hans Christian Andersen. Sophie would have loved to look at the statue because she loved his fairytales. Her grandmother read them to her when she was a child. But time was running and her group had to rush and, with the help of the coordinates, find the next place to finally find the geocache and win the race. So rush back to the last place!

17 The coordinates of this place do not match with the last information our friends got. You are at a little hut selling Belgian Waffles. They smell delicious and most people passing by have to buy one! You can get them with Belgian chocolate, cherries, cream or bananas on top. Besides, the app starts to beep which means you have found a wrong place on the map. Oh no, one step back.

18 The geocaching race is on! After they got the equipment and watched the video, they knew what to do and could finally start! Both groups walked in different directions for a little distance. Of course, they didn't want the other group to hear what they discussed! Amir, Josh and Sophie sat on a bench under a large elm to see how the tablet and app worked they had to use. "We'll manage, don't worry, I was always good at reading coordinates from a map in Geography class", Sophie said.

19 Sophie, Amir and Josh were on the Billy Johnson playground. Little children really like the playgrounds in Central Park because there are only few lawns in Manhattan. On this one there are always many children playing with their toys in the sand so that's why this would not be a good place for a geocaching activity. Please go on searching and go back to the last location.

20 After the geocaching activities the six friends walked past a small food stall decorated with pineapples, mangoes and bananas. "I can't believe it", Lauren shouted, "they are selling shave ice! We have to get some! It's delicious." "Shave ice – what's that?", everybody wondered, but of course they got some and enjoyed it on their way back to the subway. This was a really nice day and everybody was happy! The six friends would recommend geocaching no matter where, not only in Central Park!

21 Our friends were in front of the Plaza Hotel – wow what a beautiful building. Probably everybody has seen this building in a lot of films. Many people like to get married here . It is right next to Central Park but not inside. That's why it is not the correct location of the next hint, please keep on searching!

22 The memorial is named after the famous Beatles song "Strawberry Fields Forever" and so Amir, of course, started to sing immediately. Josh walked around the memorial with the tablet that suddenly vibrated with the next online clue. "That's so cool, I really like this type of treasure hunt", Josh said proudly. It turned out Sophie was pretty good at reading coordinates and finding the correct direction, therefore she led her group to the next destination: the Central Park Zoo. From far away they could hear the sounds of the zoo animals, Amir thought he must have heard some bears and penguins squeaking.

23 "So if the next one is the last place we have to find the geocache. That is usually a small container with a little something in it. I am pretty curious what will be inside!", Amir said. After 15 minutes they arrived at the point the map had shown them, the Loeb Boathouse. It took them another ten long minutes to find the location of the geocache because it was hidden under roots of an old tree. When they opened the box, they were shocked and surprised at the same time: it was empty!

My reading trail:

1													

Vocabulary

immediately	direkt	**destination**	Ziel
to squeak	quietschen, quieken	**to reveal**	erscheinen
elm	Ulme	**reward**	Belohnung, Gewinn
food stall	Essensstand	**fairytale**	Märchen
hint	Hinweis	**urgent**	dringend
competition	Wettbewerb	**ambitious**	ehrgeizig

Geocaching in Central Park
Lesespurgeschichte (2)

Last Friday, the six friends Amir, Peter, Sophie, Lauren, Hailey and Josh finally found time for an activity which was on their "to do-list" for a long time: geocaching in Central Park! Before they left, they discussed how to divide the two groups. When they were about to argue about the possible group constellations, they had the idea to draw lots and let fortune decide. It turned out that Amir, Sophie and Josh would be one team as well as Peter, Lauren and Hailey.

If you want to find out, who won the geocaching adventure and if the friends really liked it, start reading at number 1.

1 Still in the subway, Sophie was super excited and told Lauren: "I am a bit sad that we won't be in the same group. I would have loved to do this activity with you!" "Yes, me too. But let's see which team wins – I am really happy we're finally doing this!", Lauren replied. Since it was a Saturday, the subway was packed and a lot of people were heading downtown for nice activities. Our six friends could see young boys with skateboards, families with picknick baskets, people with frisbees and skates. It was a beautiful day for outdoor activities in Manhattan and explore the city. Of course, there were lots of tourists in the subway – but we're in New York!

2 Here is another famous place in Central Park and something to be found all over Manhattan: a hot dog food stall! When you're out exploring the city a hot dog can be a quick way not to starve. It's also rather cheap compared to the restaurants close to the main tourist attractions. The hot dog food stall in Central Park is always crowded and our friends also liked to quickly grab a hot dog when they were hungry. Today they didn't have time and had to postpone eating because they had to continue their search and the tablet didn't lead them here. Go back to the last location and continue the way in another direction.

3 "Sorry boys, but it was so urgent and really necessary", Sophie said while leading the group to the next place. Behind some trees she saw where their way would go: it was the Alice in Wonderland Statue! That was also one of Sophie's favourite places in Central Park since she loved the story of Alice in Wonderland and the Disney film was also part of some of her favourite childhood memories. Around the statue there were always groups of people enjoying coffee, cold drinks or ice cream probably taking a break from long walks around the huge area of Central Park. When the three friends arrived, the map showed them the coordinates for the last place!

4 The employee of the geocaching company was a nice and funny guy not older than 25, Sophie guessed. The friends explained that they had already split up in two groups and they would do a competition and see which team arrived faster! "Good idea, guys, this way geocaching is a lot more fun, you should think of a personal reward for the winners … hahaha. Of course, the winning group who finds the geocache will get OUR reward", Tom, the boss of GeocachNY, laughed. Then he handed out two tablets to them, one to Amir and one to Hailey and appointed them the leaders of the groups being responsible for the equipment. Then Tom asked them inside to watch a short introduction video.

5 "Espressooooo, Latteeee, Cappuccinooo … Regular milk, almond milk, oat milk!", a man shouted in a powerful voice. That was the famous coffee bike of an old Italian guy who loved to share his passion for good coffee. His ancestors had once brought it from Italy and passed it on to him. He often parked his coffee bike next to one of the playgrounds but sometimes you could also find him close to the pond, depending on his mood and where he expected more people to pass by. Even though he was a funny person, our friends didn't drink coffee yet and with the help of the map on their tablet they also found out that this was not the correct place. So please go on searching.

6 Once they got closer to Central Park Zoo, Josh started looking for the exact coordinates of their next POI where the following hint would be revealed. This was not easy at all and you had to be very precise. Josh got extremely passionate and ambitious after the first minutes of the geocaching race and after Sophie had explained in detail how to read the coordinates correctly. She had paid attention in geography class and had also had an excellent teacher. Their search led the three friends to the Safari Playground afterwards: a beautiful playground surrounded by trees and it got its name because there are a lot of grey hippo statues children can climb on.

In geography class in school, Sophie, Peter and the others learned how to read coordinates correctly and find places on a map. They also learned about the different states of the US.

The US is a huge country with .... states. ....

is the most recent state which joined the union in August 1959. Germany, in contrast,

has .... federal states.

7 In front of you, you can see the Great Lawn, which was always full of people playing frisbee, lying on blankets, doing a picknick or children chasing each other. It was a very nice place for a break after a long day at work or at school, an exhausting sightseeing day or just to enjoy a beautiful day with your family. Sophie knew straight away that this was no convenient spot for a geocaching location since there were so many people around and somebody could accidentally be lying at the point of interest. Players would constantly have to disturb the people here. You have to continue the search somewhere else as this is not the correct place.

8 On that little pond in the park is Gapstow Bridge. On top of the bridge you have a nice view of the skyline of Manhattan. The view of the bridge always reminded Sophie of the film "Home Alone 2 – lost in New York" and she felt a little lost – like Kevin must have felt in the film, all alone in a huge city like New York at such a young age. Today Sophie and her group did not pass the bridge and this pond since their coordinates did not tell them to. They must hurry to find the cache because they wanted to finish the activity first. Continue finding the correct way and go back to the last location.

9 "I am sure there is only one more place that we need to go to, my feeling says so", Sophie announced. "But friends, I am sorry, before we continue I urgently need to go to the toilet. Does anybody know where the public restrooms are in this park?" "Jesus, Sophie, can't you hold on until we finish the geocaching. I really want to win our competition. But alright … At the office of the company there were restrooms for the clients to use", Amir complained. "No, I CANNOT", Sophie said in a harsh tone and followed the signs for the restrooms. It took them five minutes until they arrived and then she also had to wait two or three minutes in line as there were several women queuing. When she came out, she took the tablet from Josh and followed the new directions.

10 Of course, Amir and Josh immediately climbed on two of the hippos and pretended they were cowboys riding horses and throwing lassos in the wild west. Sophie just shook her head: that childishness! She focused on the map to find the next piece of information for their search. The Safari Playground was never crowded when she was there, that was probably why it had been included in the geocaching activity, in comparison to other playgrounds that were always full of little children playing with their toys. "We need to head north … that looks as if we would be somewhere around the Delacorte Theatre", Sophie mumbled. And she was right, after a short walk they reached the theatre where a performance for kids was on. What a nice atmosphere to watch a play on a sunny day outdoors. They continued their way behind the stage of the theatre when the map revealed the next point of interest.

11 When Sophie, Amir and Josh came back to the picknick area next to the house of the geocaching company, the others were already waiting there. "Oh no, I told you, they were faster. Sophie, that's only because you had to go to the toilet and it took us so long to find the public toilets in this park. It can't be true, we lost to them!", Amir complained. Again, Sophie had to calm herself down to not shout at Amir, the idiot! "Amir, stop being such a bad loser and shouting at poor Sophie, we were just the better team. Acknowledge and accept it!", Lauren replied. "Yeah, sorry! You are right", Amir finally replied. "Sorry, Soph!" The second team told the others that in the cache there was actually nothing special. But that's normal for geocaching, it's not about the prize but the journey is the reward.

12 You arrived at the Tennis Center in Central Park which is a nice place to play tennis but it's also very expensive. Josh liked playing tennis but today they didn't have time for activities like this, the focus was on the geocaching treasure hunt! Their map told them to go in another direction and change their way. Here they were not at the correct location even though it was also interesting to look through the fence and watch the people play tennis. Some of them were really professional!

13 On their way to the address of the company Amir suddenly started to sing "It's a beautiful day … hey hey … It's a beautiful day …" And the other friends joined in and sang along while walking around New York on this beautiful summer day. "Oh no, look at the clouds up there, I hope it won't rain", Sophie said with a worried expression. "Oh Sophie, pleeeease, don't be so pessimistic, that's annoying", Amir replied. "Don't worry, Soph, I am sure it won't rain and if so, I have an umbrella that you can borrow or we'll ask the company if they have rain capes." When they passed a small kiosk, Sophie decided to buy a small umbrella – better be safe than wet on this big day!

14 Up at the subway station when the friends got out of the train, they quickly needed to check their phones to see where they could find the little house of the company that offers the geocaching tours in Central Park. They provide all the equipment you need, give you a short introduction regarding security and explain what you have to do if there is a problem. There are always employees of the company around the park who can quickly be there with their electric scooters and help you if you cannot continue. Josh found it and led the group in the correct direction.

Did you know? In British English the floor of a building at street level is called the ground floor. The floor above is the first floor and the floor below is called the basement.
In American English the floor at street level is usually called the first floor. With this information, fill in the following chart:

I live on the …	
third floor	
second floor	
first floor	
ground floor	

15 Sophie tried to stay calm after Amir's nasty remark. "Breathe, inhale, exhale", she told herself and pushed away her anger. She knew they would only lose precious time if they started to argue now. Amir and Josh were already busy trying to read the coordinates correctly and "translate" what the digital map said about

the reality they saw. "I wish I had paid more attention in geography class!!", Amir shouted frustratedly. "Let me have a look", Sophie said, took the tablet, turned it around a few times until she knew in which direction they had to go. After a few minutes walk they had to change the direction again, then they arrived at the first POI (point of interest): the strawberry fields. This is a memorial dedicated to John Lennon, the lead singer of the Beatles who was murdered in New York.

16 You are in front of the statue of the famous Danish fairytale writer Hans Christian Andersen who is not only famous in Europe but also in the US. Sophie would have loved to look at the statue closely since he loved listening to his fairytales when she was younger and her grandmother used to read them to her. These were great childhood memories. Today time was running and her group had to rush and find the next place with the help of the coordinates to finally find the geocache and win the race. So rush back to the last place!

17 The coordinates of this place do not match with the last information our friends got. Here you are at a little hut selling Belgian Waffles. They smell delicious and most people passing by cannot move on without buying one because they taste like heaven! You can get them with Belgian chocolate, cherries, cream or bananas on top. Besides, the app starts to beep which means, according to the short introduction video, you have found and marked a wrong place on the map. Oh no, one step back and the search for the next hint has to continue.

18 The geocaching race is on! After they got the equipment and watched the video, they knew what to do and could finally start! They split up in their groups and walked in different directions for a little distance. Of course, they didn't want the other group to hear what they discussed – they might steal their idea for the best strategy! Amir, Josh and Sophie sat on a bench under a large elm to accommodate with the tablet and the application they had to use. "What an advantage that I was always the worst when it came to using the atlas and reading coordinates correctly in geography class hahahah", Josh laughed. "We'll manage, don't worry, I was always good at it", Sophie answered. "Oh Sophie, an optimistic remark made by you, I don't believe it", Amir laughed.

19 Sophie, Amir and Josh were on the Billy Johnson playground. Little children really like playing on the playgrounds in Central Park because there is not much green lawn in Manhattan. It's a good way for them and their parents to get some fresh air and enjoy the feeling of being surrounded by nature. On this playground there are always many children playing with their toys in the sand. Geocachers would only disturb them and parents would probably also be worried with people constantly walking around their kids. That's why this is not the correct place, please go on searching and go back to the last location.

20 After the geocaching activities the six friends walked past a tiny food stall decorated in a tropic style with pineapples, mangoes and bananas painted on the roof. "I can't believe it", Lauren shouted, "they are selling shave ice! We have to get some! It's really delicious." "Shave ice – what's that?", everybody wondered, but of course they got some and enjoyed it immensely on their way back to the subway. This was a really nice day and everybody was happy! The six friends would recommend geocaching no matter where, not only in Central Park!

You don't know what "shave ice" is? Look it up on the internet and next time you see it: try it! It's simply delicious!

21 Our friends were in front of the Plaza Hotel – wow what a beautiful building. Probably everybody has seen this building in a lot of films, it's often used as a set location. Pure magic! Moreover, a lot of people like to get married here – some girls living in New York say they want to marry the man of their dreams in the Plaza Hotel. They would probably do everything to make this come true! The hotel is right next to Central Park but not inside. It is not the correct location of the next hint, please keep on searching!

22 Since the memorial is named after the famous Beatles song "Strawberry Fields Forever", Amir, of course, started to sing immediately. "Let me take you down cause I'm going to strawberry fields. Nothing is real …" Josh held the tablet and walked around the memorial with it when suddenly it vibrated and the next online clue appeared. "That's so cool, I really like this type of treasure hunt", Josh said proudly. It turned out Sophie was pretty good at reading coordinates and finding the correct direction, therefore she led her group to the next destination: the Central Park Zoo. From far away they could already hear the sounds of the zoo animals, Amir thought he must have heard grizzly bears roaring and penguins squeaking.

23 "So if the next one is the last place we have to find the geocache. That is usually a small cleverly hidden container with a little something in it. I am pretty curious what will be inside!", Amir said. That last walk was probably the longest of all and Josh was already getting impatient. After 15 minutes they arrived at the point the map had shown them, the Loeb Boathouse. It took them another ten long minutes to find the location of the geocache since it was definitely cleverly hidden under large root of an old tree which stuck out of the ground. When they opened the box, they were shocked and surprised at the same time: it was empty!

My reading trail:

1													

Geocaching in Central Park
Lösungen

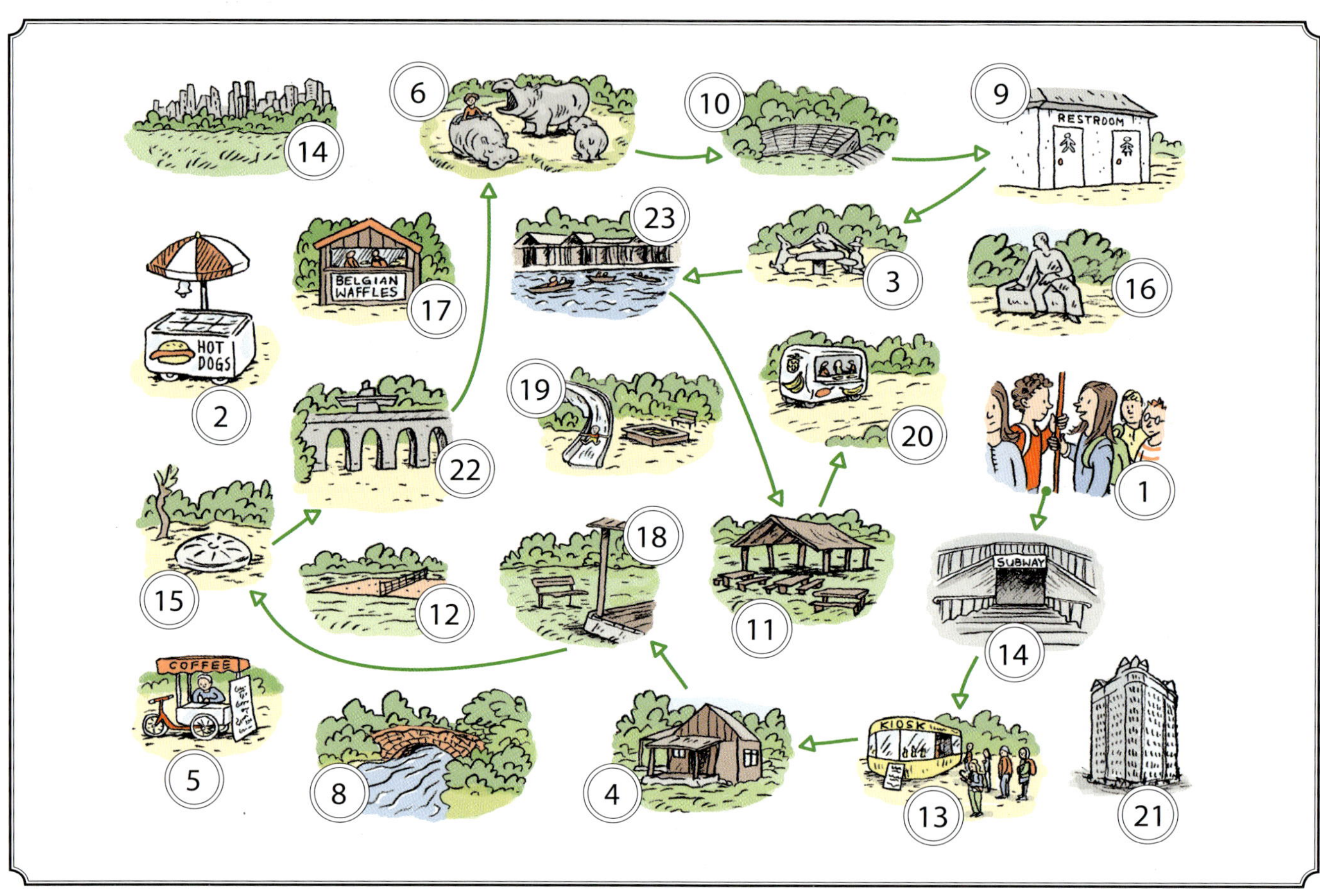

My reading trail:	1	14	13	4	18	15	22	6	10	9	3	23	11	20

Solutions:

Riddle to **6**: In geography class in school, Sophie, Peter and the others learned how to read coordinates correctly and find places on a map. Besides, they also learned about the different states of the US. The US is a huge country with **50** states. **Hawaii** is the most recent state which joined the union in August 1959. Germany, in contrast, has **16** federal states.

Riddle to **14**:

I live on the ...	
🇬🇧	🇺🇸
third floor	fourth floor
second floor	third floor
first floor	second floor
ground floor	first floor

Riddle to **20**: Shaved ice is made of fine shavings of ice or finely crushed ice and sweet condiments or syrups. Usually, the syrup is added after the ice is frozen and shaved. It is originally from Japan but is eaten a lot in Hawaii nowadays.